The Ultimate DVD Easter Egg Guide

The Ultimate DVD Easter Egg Guide

Jo Berry

ORION

Copyright © 2004 Jo Berry and
the Orion Publishing Group

The right of Jo Berry to be identified as the author
of this work has been asserted by her in accordance
with the Copyright, Designs and Patents Act 1988

First published in Great Britain in 2004 by Orion
an imprint of Orion Books Ltd
Orion House, 5 Upper St Martin's Lane,
London WC2H 9EA

A CIP catalogue record for this book is
available from the British Library

ISBN 0 75286 724 5

Printed and bound by
Clays Ltd, St Ives plc

Contents

This book is for Steve,
my very own happy ending.

Checking all the DVD Easter eggs was a mammoth task, especially as the discs themselves had to be begged, stolen and/or borrowed first. So many thanks to those who helped in the procurement of DVDs, including: Carin Shine in the press office of BBC Video, Nina Criswick at DSA for the Fox videos, the very helpful gentlemen of *Nuts* magazine (especially Iain and Ade), Karen and David, and Prime Time Video in Berwick Street. Also, thanks to Jeff Dawson.

Introduction

Welcome to the first ever guidebook to DVD Easter eggs.

Before we go any further, I'd better explain what Easter eggs are, what's in this book, and why it's a must for anyone who owns a DVD player. As the title of this book suggests, Easter eggs are something you find on DVDs, but are nothing to do with those of the chocolate variety. (Although surely someone somewhere will hopefully one day figure out the link between watching movies and scoffing calorific treats, and will devise yummy tie-ins, like putting the DVD of *Phone Booth* inside a scrumptious milk-chocolate phone-box, and including an action figure of the even more delicious Colin Farrell, too.)

The Easter eggs that appear in this book are, in fact, hidden extra features on DVDs. Of course, extras on DVDs are nothing new. Commentary from the director, interviews with members of the cast, extra scenes that were deleted from the movie's theatrical release and high-octane trailers that had advertised the movie are often all easily accessible from the disc's main menu for everyone to enjoy. But, increasingly, the producers of a DVD like to keep something else up their sleeves. An Easter egg is an extra feature, too (though often smaller and almost always quirkier than the regular extras), but it's not to be found on the menu. It's hidden so that fans have to search for it.

Don't worry, you don't have to be Albert Einstein to find an Easter egg. Sometimes they're hardly hidden at all, and may even be advertised on the DVD's box. You might be required to do something as simple as highlight a symbol on one of the disc's menus to reveal a deleted clip, an out-takes reel or an interview. Then again, you might have to press just the right combination of keys on your remote control to reveal a secret symbol, which will take you to a secret menu, which will finally allow you to see what you've been searching for over the past twenty minutes. Trickiest of all are those eggs needing access codes, where there is no hint of which number you need, and no on-screen keypad with which to enter it. Instead, you have to guess the code (take a bow *Terminator 2* for sheer imagination – it uses the date the world is supposed to end in the movie) and enter it at a specific time, which may well turn you into a fair approximation of a deranged monkey, banging your remote in an increasingly agitated fashion before you fling it across the room in frustration. Or at least that was the case before you had this book to guide you.

Mark Oates, of online magazine *DVD Reviewer* (www.dvd. reviewer.co.uk), believes that the Easter egg phenomenon has grown because 'it gives the viewer a feeling of being part of something. It's like an in joke. You know something that other people don't. For example, the Easter egg on the first of the *Star Wars* discs was very well hidden. It was a set of out-takes from the movie. They're a must-see if you're a fan of the movie, and because not many buyers of the disc would be aware of the Easter egg, if you're in the know and have been able to uncover them, you're in an exclusive little club.' Well, either an exclusive little club or a mental asylum, depending on how many times you had to tap the code 1138 – a reference to George Lucas's earlier movie, *THX1138* – into your remote before getting the gag reel to work.

Maybe I've spent too long in a darkened room alone with my TV and DVD player, but there is also a strange sense of achievement when you reveal an egg, especially the more complicated ones. This book will help you to get the satisfaction without having to go through the frustration. (I've gone through that for you, and have the frown lines to prove it!) You'll learn how to access tons of Easter eggs that have been hidden on over a hundred DVDs: not just movies, but TV series, music compilations and comedy shows.

All of the DVDs featured in the main section of this book are for **Region 2** (UK/Europe). If you have a disc that is for **Region 1** (USA), you may find that the Easter egg described here also appears on your DVD. However, that is often not the case. So don't send me angry letters if you can't access a semi-naked Halle Berry on the *Die Another Day* DVD you brought back from the US. (Quite a few DVDs only have eggs on the US and not the UK version, in fact. For those of you lucky enough to own a multi-region player, I have mentioned some of the best Region 1 eggs at the end of the book.)

Something else to look out for if a description of an egg makes you want to rush out to buy the movie is that the eggs included here are often to be found only on a specific version of the DVD. For example, the *Amelie* egg is only on the two-disc collector's version, not the single-disc version. Where this is the case, I have mentioned the version you need to buy in order to view the egg. (I say 'buy' because often the rental version of a DVD has no extras at all, let alone eggs.)

Every single one of the directions that tell you how to find the Easter eggs in this book has been tested by me, using my trusty, no-frills DVD player. On the DVD discs that I had, they *all* worked (although the 'infected DVD' on *Hitchhiker's Guide to the Galaxy* and the aforementioned *Star Wars Episode I* are particularly nightmarish to uncover, and both worked only after numerous attempts and much cursing).

This book does *not* include every movie or TV series DVD on release in the UK that features an Easter egg. I haven't included eggs that are just trailers for other movies that were released at the same time (boring!) or those eggs that are just DVD credits (a list of the people who worked on the DVD – even more boring, for anyone whose name doesn't appear in that list).

I *have* included all the DVDs I could find that contained interesting, fun or just goddamned quirky eggs lurking secretly behind the main menus. This means that there is an eclectic mix of DVD entertainment in this book, and by no means all of it is of Oscar-winning quality. So, alongside some of the best movies and TV shows ever made (*The Godfather*, *Raging Bull* and *Twin Peaks* all feature here), there are one or two that didn't exactly have the critics reaching for the thesaurus to find another superlative (*Final Destination 2* and *Not Another Teen Movie* immediately spring to mind). However, even if the film isn't up to much, if it's in this book, the egg is worth checking out.

Each individual egg has also been given a star rating from * to ***** – and remember, this is for the *egg*, not for the movie as a whole. I feel I should make this absolutely clear, because everyone will think I've completely lost my marbles (and my critical judgement) if I appear to have given *Battlefield Earth* a rating of four stars out of five. To set the record straight, I thought that film was a load of boring twaddle, with the only entertainment coming from John Travolta's hilarious haircut. The Easter egg in question was entertaining, though.

I hope you find this book useful and fun, and enjoy the Easter eggs as you uncover them. To help you on your way, check out the list of the ten best eggs on page 5. Each of them is so good, they're worth the price of the DVD all on their own.

Happy hunting!
Jo
March 04

THE TOP 10 EASTER EGGS

1 The storyboard alternative ending for **28 Days Later**

2 The interview with Quentin Tarantino on **Reservoir Dogs**

3 The black-and-white alternative beginning for **The Rocky Horror Picture Show**

4 The clip of *The Sopranos* on **The Godfather Trilogy**

5 The subtitles that help you understand Brad Pitt on **Snatch**

6 The chronological alternative version of **Memento**

7 The brief Keith Richards clip on **Pirates of the Caribbean**

8 Mr Tinkles' auditions on **Cats and Dogs**

9 The out-takes from **Star Wars Episode I: The Phantom Menace** and **Star Wars Episode II: Attack of the Clones**

10 The mini-documentary about an *Alien* fan and his Halloween costume, 'A Boy and his Powerloader', on the final disc of the **Alien Quadrilogy** box set

Honourable mention: **Moulin Rouge!**, simply for having so many Easter eggs!

Ali G, Aiii

Sacha Baron Cohen's comic creation Ali G became a TV sensation in the UK, as was made cringingly apparent when Richard Madeley felt the need to impersonate the leader of the Staines Massive on *This Morning*. This is a feature-length compilation of moments from *Da Ali G Show* (including interviews with Gail Porter and Jarvis Cocker, and a trip to the Cannes Porn Film Festival), as well as thirty minutes of extra footage of Ali G in the USA, where he interviews spokespeople for the National Rifle Association and NASA, and bumps into Paul Daniels and Peter Stringfellow.

Easter Egg

Out-take

At the Main Menu, highlight 'Play' and then press the UP arrow on your remote.

This will take you to a short clip of Sacha Baron Cohen posing as an Austrian TV presenter interviewing German band Gundog.

★ ★ ★

Alien Quadrilogy Box Set (9 Discs)

There's everything an *Alien* fan could possibly want on this nine-disc DVD collection that includes all four films (*Alien*, *Aliens*, *Alien³* and *Alien: Resurrection*), each with its own disc of extras, plus a final disc of bonus features.

Of course, it's really the first two films – Ridley Scott's 1979 *Alien* and James Cameron's 1986 *Aliens* – that are the classics of this collection. Scott's atmospheric, creepy science-fiction horror introduced us to Ripley (Sigourney Weaver, in a role originally written for a man) and the crew of the spaceship *Nostromo* led by Captain Dallas (Tom Skerritt), who come to the aid of a ship's distress signal only to discover it is deserted apart from a collection of strange alien eggs. One bursts and attaches itself to crew member Kane (John Hurt). The rest is cinematic history as an alien explodes out of his chest hours later and the remaining blood-splattered crew are then hurtled into a monster nightmare, truly deserving the infamous tagline, 'In space no one can hear you scream'.

With the alien beautifully designed by artist H. R. Giger and an iconic ass-kicking heroine in the form of Weaver, it was no surprise that the idea would be resurrected, as it was for Cameron's more action-packed *Aliens*, in which poor Ripley ends up terrorised by not one but many of these beasts, aided only by a group of marines and a small girl who has survived on the planet long after the creatures have munched on all the other residents.

Unfortunately, *Alien³* was less successful, despite being directed by David Fincher, who went on to make the superb *Se7en* and *Fight Club* (the version here is thirty minutes longer than the theatrical release he reportedly hated, and is believed to be closer to what Fincher envisaged). The story is simple: Ripley – surely now very much in need of a holiday – crash-lands on a prison planet and has to do battle alongside the shaven-headed prisoners (who all look identical, so you're never quite sure which one has just been eaten), when it turns out she has brought an alien hitch-hiker with her. Oh, and to make things even more icky, she has a baby alien gestating inside her.

Finally, rounding off the series is the visually impressive but ultimately unsatisfying *Alien: Resurrection*, from *Delicatessen*'s Jean-Pierre Jeunet, in which Ripley (who died at the end of *Alien³*) returns as a clone to do battle once more, alongside Call (Winona Ryder) and a collection of disgruntled space pirates. It's not the ending we hoped for, perhaps, but it is *an* ending to the most scary, atmospheric space horror in history.

Easter Eggs

1) A Boy And His Powerloader
Insert Disc 4 (the *Aliens* bonus disc).

At the Main Menu, select the 'Post production' menu and press ENTER.

Highlight 'The Final Countdown' and press the LEFT arrow on your remote to highlight an icon at the top right.

Press ENTER for an interview with Van Ling, who talks about how he got a job with James Cameron after building a seven-foot powerloader (a contraption from *Aliens*) for a

Halloween party. Inspiration for anyone who wants a job behind the scenes in the movies.

2) Loving The Alien

Insert Disc 8 (the *Alien: Resurrection* bonus disc).

At the Main Menu, select 'Post Production' and press ENTER.

Highlight 'More' and press ENTER.

Highlight 'Visual Effects Gallery' and then press the LEFT arrow on your remote to highlight an icon at the top right.

Press ENTER for a mini-feature on one man's dream come true of becoming an alien.

Almost Famous Untitled (Director's Edition: Extended Cut)

Former rock journalist turned moviemaker Cameron Crowe delivered a loving tribute to seventies rock with this semi-autobiographical tale of a teenage boy, William (Patrick Fugit), who gets the chance to write about his favourite rock band and follow them on tour for esteemed magazine *Rolling Stone*.

Against his mother's (Frances McDormand) objections, William befriends up-and-coming Stillwater with the help of one of the group's 'band-aids' (groupies, to you and I), the bewitchingly named Penny Lane (Kate Hudson), and accompanies them on the road in the hope of securing an interview with the band's lead guitarist, Russell (Billy Crudup).

Setting the film in 1973 (around the time Crowe himself got his start), the fictional band's antics have led many to speculate on which real-life groups provided Crowe with his inspiration. But even if you don't know your Allman Brothers from your Led Zeppelin (shame on you), and you have no idea who Lester Bangs was, this is still a fascinating, lovingly written and beautifully played ode to youth, first love (William, of course, falls for Penny) and, most important of all, music.

Easter Eggs

1) Extended Bus Scene

Insert Disc 1, select 'Special Features' from the Main Menu and press ENTER.

Highlight 'Deleted Scenes' and then press the UP arrow on your remote to highlight the underpants over William's head.

Press ENTER to see an extended version of the scene featuring the schoolgirls running alongside the bus.

★ ★ ★ ★

2) Philip Seymour Hoffman/Lester Bangs

Insert Disc 2, select 'Special Features' from the Main Menu and press ENTER.

Select 'Cameron Crowe's Top Albums of 1973' and press ENTER.

Select the arrow at the bottom of the page and press ENTER to go to the second page of Crowe's album choices.

Highlight 'Special Features' and then press the UP arrow on your remote TWICE to reveal a star symbol.

Press ENTER for a clip of Philip Seymour Hoffman as Lester Bangs, introduced by Cameron Crowe.

★ ★ ★

Amelie (2-Disc Special Edition)

An absolutely charming movie from Jean-Pierre Jeunet (*Delicatessen*), this comedy romance stars Audrey Tautou as the bashful Amelie, a young, single waitress who makes it her mission in life to bring happiness to other people – whether by instigating a romance between two regulars at the café where she works or by inspiring her father with thoughts of exotic travel.

Jeunet populates Amelie's Paris with quirky characters, including the handsome eccentric (Mathieu Kassovitz) Amelie falls for but is too shy to approach. Endearing and delightful, just like the girl herself, this is a warm and fuzzy film that invites us all to see love, life and Paris itself bathed in a dreamy, romanticised light.

Easter Egg

The Gnome's Travels

Insert Disc 2, select 'The Station' from the Main Menu and press ENTER.

Highlight 'Main Menu' and then press the DOWN arrow on your remote to highlight the gnome.

This will launch him on his journeys in the film. You will be taken to a map where you can click on the gnome's various destinations and see the snapshots he took there.

★ ★ ★

American Pie 2

This second slice of pie isn't quite as good as the first, since the novelty has worn off a bit, but there are just as many gross-out moments as the sex-obsessed boys (Jason Biggs, Chris Klein, Thomas Ian Nicholas, Seann William Scott and Eddie Kaye Thomas) hire a beach house for the summer and end up in various raunchy situations involving super glue, lesbians and an unusually positioned trumpet.

Jason Biggs, as the most unfortunate Jim (he's the one who gets too acquainted with the glue), Eugene Levy, as his dad, and Alyson Hannigan, as band camp girl Michelle, get the best gags, but the film does ultimately suffer from a lack of new ideas and is less gut-twistingly funny than the original. The DVD extras include a trailer, classic quotes and music.

Easter Egg

Cast Egg

Select 'Bonus Material' from the Main Menu and press ENTER.

Select the arrow at the bottom of the page and press ENTER to go to the second page of bonus material.

Press the UP arrow on your remote to highlight 'Bonus Materials' at the top of the page.

Press ENTER to see a silly Easter egg featuring Mena Suvari, Jason Biggs and Thomas Ian Nicholas.

★ ★ ★

Austin Powers: The Spy Who Shagged Me

Mike Myers' comic British secret agent returns for a second adventure, once again gnashing his bad teeth at arch nemesis Dr Evil (also Myers). After Austin's honeymoon with Vanessa (Elizabeth Hurley) comes to an explosive end, he discovers that Dr Evil is back and has invented a time machine so he can go back to 1969 to steal Austin's mojo, rendering him powerless in the spying and shagging departments.

Myers, who co-wrote the script with *Saturday Night Live*'s Michael McCullers, has added a few new twists to his spoof-Bond formula, including the introduction of Heather Graham as CIA agent Felicity Shagwell, and Dr Evil's creation Mini-Me, a pint-sized version of himself. Unfortunately, there are some very humourless moments featuring Myers' other new invention, the almost offensive Fat Bastard (Myers again). There are laughs to be had, but this isn't as funny as the video Myers made with Madonna for her single from the film, 'Beautiful Stranger'.

Very juvenile stuff and – rumour has it – George W. Bush's favourite film. The Special Edition DVD includes deleted scenes, music videos and the following egg.

Easter Egg

Dr Evil Special Features

Select 'Special Features' from the Main Menu and press ENTER.

At the 'Special Features' menu, wait for Mike Myers to disappear off the screen and Dr Evil's rocket to appear. When it leaves, a Dr Evil symbol will be left on the screen.

Highlight the symbol and press ENTER.

This takes you to Dr Evil's Special Features Menu, where you can see the two duets he performs with Mini-Me from the film and a few pages of Classic Evil Schemes Gone Awry (notes on plots thwarted by James Bond, Matt Helm, Harry Palmer and Derek Flint).

★ ★ ★

Note: If you own the Region 1 (US) version, the Dr Evil Special Features also includes a twenty-minute TV special on Dr Evil.

Battlefield Earth

John Travolta virtually annihilated his entire career in one go when he made this ill-advised sci-fi adventure, based on a novel by Scientology founder L. Ron Hubbard. As well as pushing for the film to be made, Travolta donned a dreadlock fright wig and scary make-up to play the lead bad-guy alien, and dragged his wife Kelly Preston in for a brief cameo, too.

Travolta's performance is actually pretty entertaining, in a so-camp-it's-good sort of way. He plays one of the aliens from the planet Psychlo who, in the year 3000, have taken over Earth and enslaved humans, including Barry Pepper, who becomes the most likely person to save the day.

Unfortunately, while Travolta storms around the grimy sets, chewing and spitting out the scenery with gusto, Pepper wavers in the background with a look of horror on his face (one assumes he has just read the script). It's all pretty disastrous, but, as with *Showgirls*, this is one of those truly bad films that is worth checking out so you can fully appreciate its awfulness.

Easter Eggs

1) Behind The Scenes

Select 'Special Features' from the Main Menu and press ENTER.

Select 'Commentary' and press ENTER.

If you now watch the film with the director's commentary,

occasionally a symbol will appear on the screen. If you press ENTER whenever it appears, you will see behind-the-scenes footage pertaining to the scene.

2) Make-up

Select 'Special Features' from the Main Menu and press ENTER.

Press the RIGHT arrow on your remote to reveal a symbol on the ship and press ENTER.

This reveals a short clip of make-up tests for the film.

3) Behind-The-Scenes Clip

Select 'Special Features' and press ENTER.

Select 'Continue' and press ENTER to go to the second page of Special Features.

Press the RIGHT arrow on your remote to reveal a symbol on the pyramid.

Press ENTER for a behind-the-scenes clip from the movie.

★ ★

4) Stunts

Select 'Special Features' and press ENTER.

Select 'Continue' and press ENTER to go to the second page of Special Features.

Select 'Cast & Crew' and press ENTER.

Highlight 'Features' and press the UP arrow on your remote to reveal a symbol.

Press ENTER for a short stunt clip.

5) More Stunts

Select 'Languages' from the Main Menu and press ENTER.

Highlight 'Off' and press the RIGHT arrow on your remote to reveal a symbol.

Press ENTER for another stunt clip.

★ ★

Being John Malkovich

One of the most inventive Hollywood movies of the nineties, this comedy/drama/bizarre trip tells the story of Craig Schwartz (John Cusack), a puppeteer barely making ends meet who takes a filing job in a strange company on the $7^1/_2$th floor of a big city building. One day, Craig discovers that behind one of the office cabinets is a door, and when he goes through it he discovers it is some sort of metaphysical portal that sends him lurching into the brain of actor John Malkovich, allowing him to experience the things Malkovich does for fifteen minutes before expelling Craig onto the side of the New Jersey Turnpike.

Writer Charlie Kaufman cleverly weaves an intricate plot around this outstanding idea, beginning when Craig lets colleague Maxine (Catherine Keener) in on his discovery and she convinces him to charge people to try this demented ride for themselves.

Director Spike Jonze beautifully translates this smart, subversive and darkly comic tale to the screen with help from the terrific cast, most notably Cusack and an almost unrecognisable Cameron Diaz as his dowdy wife. But best of all, of course, is John Malkovich himself, who parodies the public image of himself brilliantly, especially in a hilarious scene when he tries the portal himself and ends up in his own bizarre world, eating dinner in a restaurant populated by numerous Mr Malkoviches.

Easter Egg

Music

This is a semi-Easter egg – if you choose 'Language' from the
Main Menu and press ENTER, you will hear Björk's song for the
movie in its entirety.

Best of Bowie (2 Discs)

If there was ever an artist who understood the power of performance, and the impact of the music video, it must be David Bowie, that Thin White Duke who changed his persona from Ziggy Stardust to bleach-blond suit to rock elder statesman over three inventive musical decades.

This DVD has all the classic Bowie videos – the barking 'Ashes to Ashes', with Bowie wandering around on a beach in a Pierrot outfit accompanied by, among others, Steve Strange; the exotic 'China Girl'; and Julien Temple's flashy 'Blue Jean' among them – as well as early performances on *The Old Grey Whistle Test* and chat show *Russell Harty Plus Pop*.

Easter Eggs

1) Bowie on Russell Harty

Insert Disc 1, select 'Tracklisting' and press ENTER.

Highlight 'Drive in Saturday' and then press the RIGHT arrow on your remote. This reveals a line by the track name.

Press ENTER for a clip of David Bowie being interviewed by Russell Harty in 1973.

★ ★ ★ ★

2) Ziggy Stardust And The Spiders From Mars

On Disc 1, select 'Tracklisting' and press ENTER.

Select 'next' and press ENTER to go to the second page of tracks.

Highlight 'Ziggy Stardust' and press the RIGHT arrow on your remote to highlight the lightning symbol.

Press ENTER for a poster advertising *Ziggy: The Motion Picture*.

★

3) Blue Jean Extended Video

On Disc 1, select 'Tracklisting' and press ENTER.

Select 'next' and press ENTER to go to the second page of tracks.

Select 'next' and press ENTER to go to the third page of tracks.

Highlight 'Blue Jean' and press the RIGHT arrow on your remote to reveal ')'.

Press ENTER and the bottom left-hand photo will change from a still of the original Julien Temple-directed video to one of Bowie wearing sunglasses.

Press the RIGHT arrow on your remote and the alternative video – a twenty-minute extended version – will play.

★ ★ ★ ★

4) Blue Jean Alternative MTV Video

Select the Blue Jean Extended Video as above.

During the video, the girl selects 'Jazzin for Blue Jean' from the pub jukebox.

When Bowie appears on the TV screen above and sings the words 'Blue Jean', press ENTER.

A white line appears around the TV and you will see the video Bowie shot of the song for MTV.

★ ★ ★

5) Oh! You Pretty Things Alternative Take

On Disc 1, select 'Tracklisting' and press ENTER.

Select 'Oh! You Pretty Things' and press ENTER for the version of the song that Bowie recorded for *The Old Grey Whistle Test*.

Return to the Main Menu and select 'Play All'.

You will now see another version of Bowie's performance for *Whistle Test* that was never broadcast.

★ ★ ★

6) Miracle Goodnight Alternative Version

Insert Disc 2, select 'Tracklisting' and press ENTER.

Leave the first list of tracks on screen and do not touch your remote.

After approximately four minutes, an alternative version of the 'Miracle Goodnight' video, directed by Matthew Rolston, will play.

★ ★ ★

7) Seven Years In Tibet Mandarin Version

On Disc 2, select 'Tracklisting' and press ENTER.

Select 'next' and press ENTER to go to the second page of tracks.

Select 'Seven Years in Tibet' and press ENTER.

A title page appears before the video, featuring a Mandarin subtitle.

Press ENTER while this is onscreen and you will be taken to a Mandarin version of the song.

★ ★ ★

Black Hawk Down (2 Discs)

Director Ridley Scott followed up the phenomenally successful *Gladiator* (and the rather lacklustre *Hannibal*) with this war drama based on true events that occurred during the American siege of Mogadishu in 1993 – a short mission (the US soldiers should have returned after less than an hour) that turned into a day of urban warfare after two Black Hawk helicopters crashed and the troops in them had to fight to survive on the streets under fire from Somalian troops.

Scott assembled an impressive cast – Tom Sizemore, Ewan McGregor, Sam Shepard, Jason Isaacs and Josh Hartnett among them – as the officers, but the star here is really Scott himself, who depicts the chaos, bloody carnage, street fire-fights and crashes with gritty, horrific realism that is all the more powerful when he reminds us that during this battle the US army suffered its worst losses since the Vietnam War.

Easter Egg

Dos And Don'ts

Insert Disc 1, select 'Special Features' and press ENTER.

Select 'Commentaries' and press ENTER.

Highlight 'On' for author Mark Bowden and screenwriter Ken Nolan's commentary.

Press the LEFT arrow on your remote to reveal a yellow door.

Press ENTER for Nolan's funny notes on how to do a decent commentary for DVD.

★ ★ ★

Buffy the Vampire Slayer: Season Six (DVD Collection)

One of the most original TV series to come out of the USA in the nineties, *Buffy the Vampire Slayer* told – over seven seasons (ending in 2003) – the story of a teenage girl named Buffy (Sarah Michelle Gellar) who was selected to be 'the chosen one' – a slayer of the vampires and demons who seem in endless supply in her Californian home of Sunnydale.

Cleverly realised by creator Joss Whedon as a show about a teenager that garnered a grown-up, cult audience, and wittily performed by a strong cast that included Brit Anthony Stewart Head as Buffy's watcher, Giles, *American Pie*'s Alyson Hannigan as witchy Willow, Nicholas Brendon as Xander and James Marsters as punk-haired vampire Spike, by the sixth season the 'Buffyverse' (as fans dub the Buffy universe) had progressed to the point where Buffy had gained a sister (Dawn), lost a vampire lover (Angel, who gained his own spin-off series) and died twice (the second time at the end of the previous season).

The sixth-season box set features, among its highlights, the opening episode, in which Willow attempts to bring Buffy back from the dead using magic, a growing attraction between Buffy and her former nemesis Spike, and one of the most acclaimed episodes in the show's history, 'Once More with Feeling', a musical episode packed with song and dance numbers written by Whedon for his cast. (The extras on the disc featuring this episode include a funny 'making of' the musical, and Buffy karaoke so fans can sing along with the cast.)

Easter Eggs

1) Once More With Feeling CD Signing

Insert Disc 2.

Select the 'Once More with Feeling' episode from the Main Menu and press ENTER.

Select 'Language Selection' from the 'Once More with Feeling' menu and press ENTER.

On the 'Language Selection' menu, highlight 'Resume Episode' and then press the UP arrow on your remote.

This should reveal a Buffy logo. Press ENTER.

You will then be treated to a two-minute clip of Amber Benson (Tara), Michelle Trachtenberg (Dawn) and creator Joss Whedon signing CD soundtracks of the 'Once More with Feeling' musical episode at Tower Records in LA. More interesting, perhaps, are the more obsessive Buffy fans interviewed who have queued up to meet them.

★ ★ ★

2) Normal Again Call Sheet

Insert Disc 4.

Select any episode from the Main Menu and press ENTER.

Select 'Language Selection' from that episode's menu and press ENTER.

On the 'Language Selection' menu, highlight 'Resume Episode' and then press the UP arrow on your remote.

This should reveal a Buffy logo. Press ENTER.

There is now a page of instructions on how to access the call sheet for the episode 'Normal Again' on your PC. If you have a

PC with a DVD-Rom drive, you can access the call sheet directly by inserting Disc 4 into your PC and accessing the main disc directory. Within is the call sheet, as the file Buffy6_Callsheet.jpg.

★ ★

Cats and Dogs

A mixture of live action, animatronics and computer animation adds up to this entertaining family tale of felines and canines who, when they're not chasing string or burying bones, are secretly going head to head in a battle for world domination.

The cats are led by the nefarious Mr Tinkles (voiced by *Will & Grace*'s Sean Hayes), while the special-agent dogs fighting to keep world peace include Butch (voiced by Alec Baldwin), Ivy (Susan Sarandon) and new young recruit Lou (Tobey Maguire).

On the human side, there's Jeff Goldblum and Elizabeth Perkins, but the most enjoyable scenes of this thinly plotted but often funny tale come when Mr Tinkles purrs across the screen. And could his scathing line, 'Evil does not wear a bonnet!' in response to his frilly attire, be one of the best movie lines of 2001?

The DVD – in which each viewer has to choose allegiance to Cats or Dogs before accessing the Main Menu – includes a commentary, trailers, storyboards and a short documentary.

Easter Eggs

1) Mr Tinkles' Auditions

When the disc loads on your DVD, you will be given the choice of 'Cats' or 'Dogs' – choose 'Cats' and press ENTER.

Select 'Special Features' from the 'Cats' Main Menu and press ENTER.

Highlight 'HBO First Look Special' and then press the DOWN arrow on your remote to highlight the spiky ball on the screen.

Press ENTER to view a hilarious collection of some of Mr Tinkles early auditions.

★ ★ ★ ★ ★

2) Mr Tinkles: Movie Critic

At the start, choose 'Cats' as above and press ENTER.

Select 'Special Features' from the 'Cats' Main Menu and press ENTER.

Select 'Continue' at the bottom of the page and press ENTER.

Highlight 'Theatrical Trailer' and then press the DOWN arrow on your remote to highlight the Cat logo.

Press ENTER for a clip of Mr Tinkles talking about the state of movies today.

★ ★ ★ ★

3) Concept Sketches

When the disc loads on your DVD, you will be given the choice of 'Cats' or 'Dogs' – choose 'Dogs' and press ENTER.

Select 'Special Features' from the 'Dogs' Main Menu and press ENTER.

Highlight 'HBO First Look Special' and then press the DOWN arrow on your remote to highlight the tube on the screen.

Press ENTER to view some of the concept sketches for the movie.

★ ★ ★

4) Doggie Clips

At the start, choose 'Dogs' as above and press ENTER.

Select 'Special Features' from the 'Dogs' Main Menu and press ENTER.

Select 'Continue' at the bottom of the page and press ENTER.

Highlight 'Theatrical Trailer' and then press the DOWN arrow on your remote to highlight the Dog logo.

Press ENTER for some clips from the movie that prove 'dogs rule'.

★ ★ ★

Charlie's Angels

Take a 1970s TV series featuring three leading roles for the ladies, update it for the twenty-first century, throw in a music-video director (McG) and some tight costumes and you get 2000's *Charlie's Angels*, starring Drew Barrymore, Lucy Liu and Cameron Diaz as the high-kicking, ass-wiggling Angels, who solve crime at the behest of the mysterious Charlie (voiced, as in the TV series, by John Forsythe).

As you'd expect, it's glossy, fast-paced fun, like a men's magazine come to life on the screen. There's some sort of plot involving a kidnapped software genius, and Crispin Glover wanders around once in a while looking menacing, but don't expect too much in the dialogue or brains department (especially as the script was rumoured to have been written by a whopping eighteen writers) – this is eye candy for the boys, a daft but enjoyable popcorn flick for the girls.

Easter Eggs

1) The Angels

Select 'Extra Features' and press ENTER.

Highlight 'Welcome To Angel World' and then press the RIGHT arrow on your remote to highlight 'Extra Features' at the top of the page.

Press ENTER for a short clip of the three Angels tossing their hair.

2) Drew Barrymore

Select 'Extra Features' and press ENTER.

　　Select the arrow at the bottom of the page and press ENTER to go to the second page of Extra Features.

　　Highlight 'Wired Angels' and then press the LEFT arrow on your remote to highlight 'Extra Features' at the top of the page.

　　Press ENTER for a short clip of Drew Barrymore having a plaster cast made of her face.

★ ★ ★

3) Behind The Scenes

Select 'Extra Features' and press ENTER.

　　Select the arrow at the bottom of the page and press ENTER to go to the second page of Extra Features.

　　Select the right arrow at the bottom of the page and press ENTER to go to the third page of Extra Features.

　　Highlight the arrow at the bottom of the page and then press the RIGHT arrow on your remote to highlight 'Extra Features' at the top of the page.

　　Press ENTER for a series of behind-the-scenes clips, including Sam Rockwell's spot-on impersonation of Christopher Walken.

★ ★ ★ ★

Confessions of a Dangerous Mind

TV heart-throb turned accomplished film actor George Clooney directed this fascinating drama based on the autobiography of Chuck Barris, the American game-show host who claims he was also a CIA agent.

Sam Rockwell is superb as Barris, who rose to fame in the sixties as the creator and host of *The Dating Game* (a precursor to the UK's *Blind Date*) and *The Gong Show*. Often criticised in the US press for bringing trash to American TV screens, he was seen in a whole new light when he published his 'unauthorised' autobiography, in which he claimed that while he was chaperoning winners on their foreign dates for *The Dating Game*, he was carrying out hits under instruction from the CIA.

Clooney co-stars as the government agent who recruits Barris, while his pals Drew Barrymore (as Barris's long-suffering girlfriend), Julia Roberts (having fun in a small role as a spy) and, in brief cameos, Matt Damon and Brad Pitt pop up as the story zips along. Charlie Kaufman's script captures the humour and the darkness of Barris (how else could you describe a man who has such bizarre delusions?), while Clooney delivers a fascinating, off-the-wall and gripping directorial debut.

Easter Egg

George Clooney

Select 'Bonus Material' from the Main Menu and press ENTER.

Highlight 'Main Menu' and then press the LEFT arrow on your remote to reveal a square under the words 'Bonus Material'.

Press ENTER for a clip of George Clooney encouraging the cast to dance on the set of *The Gong Show*.

★ ★ ★ ★

Daredevil (2-Disc Special Edition)

Although he's probably more famous for his ex-girlfriends (Gwyneth Paltrow, Jennifer Lopez) than his career, Ben Affleck does occasionally make enjoyable movies like this fun – if thinly plotted – adventure based on the comic book of the same name. He stars as Matt Murdock, a lawyer blinded by some toxic goo as a child who discovers his other senses are heightened to the point that he can be a bit of a superhero, taking revenge on the evil and saving the helpless when he isn't doing important things with his legal briefs.

While Affleck, quite frankly, looks a bit of a berk in his red leather ensemble (and modified white cane that doubles as a weapon – *cool!*), it's the supporting cast that give the film its fun feel: *Alias'* Jennifer Garner as the knife-wielding, ass-kicking Elektra; an underused Jon Favreau as Matt's pal; and, best of all, a snarling, eye-rolling, scene-stealing Colin Farrell as psychotic killer-for-hire Bullseye.

The two-disc DVD features (as well as the following egg) a 'making of' documentary, director's commentary and music videos from the movie's soundtrack.

Easter Egg

Daredevil Out-takes

Insert Disc 2.

Select 'The Film' from the Main Menu and press ENTER.

Select 'Beyond Hell's Kitchen: The Making of Daredevil' and press ENTER.

Highlight 'Access Enhanced Viewing Mode' and then press the LEFT arrow on your remote.

This will reveal a pair of crossed knives (sais, like the ones used by Elektra in the film). Press ENTER.

A five-minute collection of gaffes and out-takes featuring the film's stars (Ben Affleck, Colin Farrell, Jennifer Garner and Jon Favreau) will now play. And it's a scream – from Ben and Jennifer trying to pull off a fight stunt to Colin Farrell landing a kiss on a surprised female co-star.

★ ★ ★ ★

Depeche Mode: One Night in Paris (2 Discs)

One of the best rock/pop bands of the eighties and nineties, Depeche Mode went on tour with their *Exciter* album in 2001, and one gig in Paris was captured on film by their long-time collaborator, photographer/music-video director Anton Corbijn.

This live video includes old and newer DM hits, including 'Enjoy the Silence', 'Black Celebration' and 'Personal Jesus', and captures Martin Gore, Dave Gahan and Andy Fletcher as they whip the Parisian crowd into a frenzy.

The second disc includes backstage clips, interviews, a bonus track and Anton Corbijn's photos from the tour.

Easter Egg

Hidden Song

Insert Disc 2, select 'The Screening' from the Main Menu and press ENTER.

Highlight 'In Your Room' and then press the RIGHT arrow on your remote three times.

The face on the left will smile and the eyes turn red. Press ENTER.

This reveals a clip of Martin Gore rehearsing 'Surrender' while applying his make-up backstage.

Die Another Day (2-Disc Special Edition)

Pierce Brosnan – a.k.a. the best Bond since Sean Connery – returns for a fourth outing as 007 in this adventure that was released just as the franchise celebrated its fortieth year. This time round, our man with a licence to kill has been captured by North Koreans and held captive, but once he is released he's barely shaved off his beard and put on one of his suave suits before he's dashing off to seek revenge.

Helping him – along with Judi Dench's M, of course – is American agent Jinx (Halle Berry, who's tougher and sexier than the Bond girls that have gone before), while Madonna pops up for an embarrassing cameo (which matches her embarrassing theme song nicely). The real star, as always with Bond movies, is the action – a car chase across ice is particularly impressive – and director Lee Tamahori packs the screen with twists and explosions to the point that even the bad guy (Toby Stevens) is left confused as to his motives.

Not a classic Bond, perhaps, but it's certainly a flashy one. The DVD includes commentaries, storyboards, trivia, Madonna's video (oh well, never mind) and documentaries.

Easter Egg

Halle Berry

Insert Disc 2 and go to the Main Menu.

Select 'Image Database' and press ENTER.

Select 'Sets and Locations' and press ENTER.

Using the RIGHT arrow on your remote, go through the pictures in this gallery until you reach the seventh, which is of Halle Berry.

Press ENTER and you can view the scene of Halle emerging from the ocean, in homage to Ursula Andress' entrance in *Dr No*, from three different angles (press 1, 2 or 3 on your remote for the different angles, or 4 to see all simultaneously). This clip is looped so you can watch it over and over, should you wish...

★ ★ ★ ★

Die Hard
(Special Edition)

Bruce Willis went from wise-cracking TV star (*Moonlighting*) to megastar thanks to the success of this blockbuster in 1988.

He plays John McClane, a smart-talking New York cop visiting his estranged wife (Bonnie Bedelia) in LA, who arrives at her office just as terrorists, led by ruthless Hans Gruber (Alan Rickman), take over the building. Luckily, our hero was in the bathroom at the time, so while the office workers (staying late for the Christmas party) are herded into a room and kept hostage by Gruber's gunmen, John sneaks away to run around the tower and foil the bad guys' plans.

Packed with smart one-liners and non-stop action as our anti-hero (he smokes, he curses and he has no qualms about dispatching the terrorists in the bloodiest ways possible) becomes, in his own words, 'a fly in the ointment, a monkey in the wrench, a pain in the ass', this is a true rollercoaster ride punctuated by explosions, fights and impressive stunts. It's hard to imagine anyone else in the role, but believe it or not, director John McTiernan originally considered Arnold Schwarzenegger for the part, having recently directed him in *Predator*. Thankfully, Bruce got the role, and went on to get his vest dirty all over again in two thoroughly enjoyable sequels.

Easter Eggs

1) In-joke

Insert Disc 2.

When the Main Menu appears onscreen, highlight 'From the Vault' and then press the RIGHT arrow on your remote.

This highlights a spot on the right of the menu.

Press ENTER to see the roof of the Nakatomi Plaza explode and a message from Fox Video (their offices were in the building that doubled as Nakatomi Plaza in the movie).

★ ★

2) Instrumental Out-takes

On disc 2, select 'From the Vault' from the Main Menu and press ENTER.

Select 'Outtakes' and press ENTER.

Select 'The Vault' and press ENTER.

Highlight 'Production Audio Only', then press the UP arrow on your remote to reveal a gun.

Press ENTER for a series of out-takes and clips featuring music from the film (and no dialogue). These are the same out-takes you can select from 'The Vault' menu with dialogue.

★ ★ ★

Die Hard with a Vengeance (2-Disc Collector's Edition)

Bruce Willis returned as his most popular character, wrong-place-at-the-wrong-time cop John McClane, for the third time in this 1995 action adventure, which also reunited him with the original *Die Hard* director John McTiernan.

Now separated from his annoying wife (sorry, Bonnie Bedelia, but you were), McClane is back in New York and this time caught up in a bomber's deadly game that begins with our hero having to stand on a Harlem street corner wearing a sandwich-board that will not exactly endear him to the local community. Luckily, local shopkeeper Zeus (Samuel L. Jackson) comes to his aid, and soon the pair are racing around Manhattan at the behest of mysterious baddie Simon (Jeremy Irons, delivering more ham than a butcher's van), unaware that their heroics are actually a cunning distraction while the bad guys go about their nefarious business.

Based on a script ('Simon Says') that was once considered as a possible sequel to *Lethal Weapon*, this isn't as inventive as *Die Hard*, and the plot has a few holes towards the end, but it's frenetic and fun, packed with one-liners and Willis's patented sarcastic charm.

Easter Egg

Gag Reel

Insert Disc 2, select 'Interview and Profile' from the Main Menu and press ENTER.

Highlight 'Interview with Bruce Willis' and then press the LEFT arrow on your remote to highlight the EXIT sign.

Press ENTER for a series of out-takes from the movie.

Doctor Who

It began in 1963 – a science-fiction adventure for the BBC packed with cheap props and wobbly sets that became a landmark cult favourite, running for over twenty-five years. Even people who have never watched an episode know who the Doctor was – a time traveller who zipped about in the Tardis, which resembled a police phone-box – and can recognise his most famous foes, the Cybermen and, of course, the Daleks (impressively, for aliens who can't even go upstairs, they have their own entry in the Oxford English Dictionary).

The BBC have released many of the episodes on DVD, including the ones below that feature Easter eggs. There's the 'Dalek Invasion of Earth', featuring the first Doctor (William Hartnell), 'Tomb of the Cybermen', with his successor (Patrick Troughton), Jon Pertwee in 'Spearhead from Space', the irreplaceable Tom Baker in 'The Ark in Space' and Peter Davison in 'Resurrection of the Daleks'.

Easter Eggs (listed by episode disc)

1) Resurrection of the Daleks
Select 'Special Features' from the Main Menu.
    Highlight 'BBC Trailer' and press the LEFT arrow on your remote.
    This highlights a Doctor Who logo, press ENTER.
    This reveals the episode countdown screen.

★ ★

2) Spearhead from Space

Highlight 'Play All' and then press the LEFT arrow on your remote to highlight the Doctor Who logo.

Press ENTER for an extended opening credits sequence.

★ ★ ★

3) The Ark in Space

Select 'Special Features' from the Main Menu and press ENTER.

Highlight 'Tom Baker Interview' and press the LEFT arrow on your remote to reveal a Doctor Who logo.

Press ENTER for a clip of Tom Baker advertising a Doctor Who exhibition.

★ ★ ★

4) Tomb of the Cybermen egg 1

On the Main Menu, highlight 'Play All' and then press the UP arrow on your remote to highlight the Doctor Who logo.

Press ENTER for a longer version of the opening credits.

★ ★ ★

5) Tomb of the Cybermen egg 2

On the Main Menu, highlight 'Play All'.

Press the UP arrow on your remote (highlighting Doctor Who logo), then the RIGHT arrow, then the LEFT arrow, to reveal a circle around the photo of Patrick Troughton.

Press ENTER for a scene from the episode which has been restored.

★ ★ ★

6) Tomb of the Cybermen egg 3

Select 'Special Features' from the Main Menu and press ENTER.

Select the arrow at the bottom of the page and press ENTER to go to the second page of Special Features.

Select 'Audio Options' and press ENTER.

Press the LEFT arrow on your remote to highlight the Doctor Who logo.

Press ENTER for an audio trailer for 'Doctor Who and the Abominable Snowman'.

★ ★ ★

7) The Dalek Invasion of Earth egg 1

Insert Disc 2.

On the Main Menu, highlight 'Talking Daleks' and then press the LEFT arrow on your remote to reveal a Doctor Who logo.

Press ENTER for a fun clip of the monster known as 'Sid'.

★ ★ ★ ★

8) The Dalek Invasion of Earth egg 2

On the Main Menu, select the arrow at the bottom of the page and press ENTER to go to the second menu page.

Highlight 'Photo Gallery' and press the LEFT arrow on your remote to reveal a Doctor Who logo.

Press ENTER for a clip of 'Sid's Date'.

Donnie Darko

Simply one of the most original movies of recent times, *Donnie Darko* is a superb mix of fantasy, drama, science fiction, comedy and even horror that is even more remarkable as it is the debut feature from writer/director Richard Kelly.

Donnie (Jake Gyllenhaal) is an average teenage boy in 1988 – except that he has a habit of sleepwalking and waking up in the middle of a road or on the local golf course. In his most recent dream, Donnie is visited by a six-foot-tall rabbit named Frank who tells him that the world will end in 28 days, 6 hours and 42 minutes. When Donnie returns home (having woken up outside again), he discovers that the engine of a plane has crashed into his family's house, smashing his bedroom.

That's just the beginning of a story that encompasses time travel, a teen romance, the local self-help guru (Patrick Swayze), a talent contest and everyday school life as Donnie slowly goes off the rails burdened with his unique knowledge and belief that more strange things are going on around him.

Gyllenhaal gives a wonderfully melancholic performance as Donnie, and is ably supported by a cast that includes his real-life sister Maggie (as Donnie's older sister), Mary McDonnell (as his Stephen King-reading mom), Noah Wyle and Drew Barrymore (as two of his teachers). A spooky, unnerving, inventive and amazing film.

Easter Eggs

1) Deleted Scenes

On the Main Menu, highlight 'Special Features' and then press the RIGHT arrow on your remote.

You will see a small rabbit appear in Frank's eye and then you will be taken to a deleted scene from the end of the movie.

If you leave the scene running, it will be repeated with audio commentary from the director. As this plays, a white rabbit appears in the corner of the screen. Press ENTER for a second deleted scene of Donnie carving pumpkins.

★ ★ ★ ★

2) More Deleted Scenes

Select 'Special Features' from the Main Menu and press ENTER.

Select 'Commentaries and Subtitles' and press ENTER.

Highlight 'Spanish Subtitles' and then press the RIGHT arrow on your remote to reveal a rabbit over Patrick Swayze's eye.

An extended scene with Donnie and his psychiatrist will now play.

The scene will then replay with a commentary. Wait for the white rabbit to appear on the screen near the end and press ENTER.

You will now see another extended scene.

Duran Duran: Greatest

The eighties pop scene wouldn't have been the same without Duran Duran – their stylish pop, complete with baffling lyrics (what, pray tell, is 'dancing on the valentine'?), those scary, spiky haircuts (we mean you, Nick Rhodes), and, of course, those luscious, expensive, foreign-location videos for 'Rio', 'Hungry Like the Wolf' and 'Union of the Snake'.

All those videos are included in this DVD collection of Duran's best-known musical moments. There's the mad 'Wild Boys' video that was filled with bald-headed creatures who looked like they had wandered off the set of some bad eighties horror movie and ended up with the Brummie band by mistake. (During the filming of this video, Simon Le Bon was attached to a bizarre windmill contraption that went underwater and he nearly drowned.) Then we have the uncensored version of 'Girls on Film', complete with – *shock, horror!* – writhing ladies, 'The Reflex', and later, lesser-seen videos for 'All She Wants Is' and 'Skin Trade'. In fact, pretty much every video they ever made is here to remind us all what a perfect pop package they were (and still are).

Easter Eggs

1) Hidden Videos
Insert Disc 1.

Go to the menu that lists music videos including 'Union of the Snake'.

Put the cursor by 'Union of the Snake' and then press the LEFT arrow on your remote.

This will reveal the outline of a man. Press ENTER.

You will now see the 'Dancing on the Valentine' version of the 'Union of the Snake' video, which is slightly different from the original.

★ ★ ★

You can also watch alternative versions of some of the other videos (though not strictly Easter eggs), as follows:

'Girls on Film' – After watching the uncensored version, select the video again and you will see the same video but with an alternative ending.

'New Moon on Monday' – Each time you select the track you will see a different version of the video (there are four).

'Wild Boys' – The 'Long Arena' version plays alternately with the original single version.

2) Hidden Interviews And Videos

On Disc 1, go to the 'Gallery' featuring Duran Duran album covers on the walls and select the following:

Highlight the 'A View to a Kill' sleeve and press ENTER.

Move cursor to PLAY and then press the RIGHT arrow on your remote.

This will highlight a spot by the title. Press ENTER and you will see a short interview with the band talking about making the Bond theme.

★ ★ ★

Highlight the 'Wild Boys' single sleeve and press ENTER so it is the main sleeve on the page.

Move cursor to PLAY and then press the UP arrow on your remote.

This will highlight a spot by the title. Press ENTER for an interview by Paul Gambaccini with Roger Taylor, Andy Taylor and Simon Le Bon.

★ ★

When you have the 'Seven and the Ragged Tiger' album sleeve on screen, move cursor to NEXT.

Press the UP arrow on your remote to reveal a spot and then press ENTER for clips of Simon Le Bon and Nick Rhodes talking about recording the album.

★ ★ ★

Select the *Duran Duran* album cover and press ENTER.

Use the DOWN arrow to select the 'Planet Earth' cover on the left and press ENTER.

Highlight the bottom square (the 'Girls on Film' sleeve) and press the LEFT arrow on your remote to reveal a spot by the 'Planet Earth' title.

Press ENTER for a 'Planet Earth' video featuring the very youthful band (as they were then) performing in a club.

★ ★ ★ ★

On Disc 2, go to the 'Gallery' featuring Duran Duran album covers on the walls and select the following:

Select the *Liberty* album cover and press ENTER.

Highlight the top single sleeve on the left-hand side and then press the UP arrow on your remote to reveal a spot.

Press ENTER to see Nick, Simon and John talking about rehearsals for Duran Duran's 1988 tour.

★ ★ ★

Select the *Liberty* album cover and press ENTER.

Select the 'Serious' single sleeve and press ENTER.

Put the cursor by the album and press the RIGHT arrow on your remote to reveal a spot.

Press ENTER to view the 'Serious' video with three additional screens featuring different camera angles.

★ ★ ★

Select the *Wedding Album* cover and press ENTER.

Highlight NEXT and press the DOWN arrow on your remote to reveal a spot.

Press ENTER for a TV advert for the *Wedding Album*, voiced by the late Paula Yates.

Select the *Wedding Album* cover and press ENTER.

Select the 'Come Undone' single sleeve and press ENTER.

Move the cursor to PLAY and then press the LEFT arrow key on your remote.

Press ENTER to view the censored version of the 'Come Undone' music video.

★ ★ ★

The Evil Dead
(Special Edition)

Now regarded as more of a horror comedy than a hide-behind-the-sofa-until-it's-over chiller, *The Evil Dead* was considered quite gruesome back in 1981, to the extent that when it came out on video in Britain it was deemed a 'video nasty'.

Now, of course, it is a huge cult hit, and deservedly so. Made on a shoestring by director Sam Raimi and his buddies, the film set a new tone for horror movies, mixing deliciously bad-taste gore with a juvenile sense of humour, and featuring characters so wholesome you actually can't wait for them to be turned into zombies or ripped limb from limb.

Bruce Campbell, a long-time friend of Raimi's, stars as Ash, who goes to a cabin in the woods with some pals for a nice weekend. But their rustic idyll is soon shattered when devils are reawakened, the woods come alive, and the evil dead pop up to munch on the terrified humans. It's almost as diabolically funny as it is blood-splatteringly yucky – much credit due to Campbell's eccentric performance – and the effects (decaying zombies and the like) are impressive, especially considering the minuscule budget.

The Special Edition DVD, which features documentaries, out-takes, trailers and TV ads, mentions the two Easter eggs below on the box. The eggs are also featured on the Limited Edition *Book of the Dead* version.

Easter Eggs

1) Make-up Test

From the Main Menu, select 'Extras' and press ENTER.

'Trailer' will be highlighted – press the LEFT arrow on your remote to highlight the demon to the left.

Press ENTER to show a make-up test for one of the demons. Ugh.

★ ★ ★

2) Panel Discussion

From the Main Menu, select 'Extras' and press ENTER.

Select 'More' and press ENTER.

'Fanalysis' will be highlighted – press the LEFT arrow on your remote to highlight the skull to the left.

Press ENTER for the panel discussion that followed a twentieth-anniversary screening of the movie on Halloween 2001.

★ ★ ★ ★

The Fast and the Furious

Take the plot of *Point Break* – young cop goes undercover to catch cool bad guys and ends up befriending the possible leader of their gang – add a pounding soundtrack, attractive cast and lots and lots of car chases, and you have *The Fast and the Furious*.

Paul Walker is said cop, who infiltrates a gang of street racers suspected of hijacking trucks. The gang is led by super-cool Vin Diesel (whose gravelly voice and impressive physique steal the show from bland pretty-boy Walker), who may or may not be up to no good. But forget the plot and concentrate instead on the flashy, well-executed car chases and stunts, edited like an MTV rock video, as the boys use their shiny vehicles to prove who has the most testosterone.

The DVD includes a commentary from director Rob Cohen, a 'making of' featurette and feature on editing.

Easter Eggs

1) Extended Car Stunt

Select 'Special Features' from the Main Menu and press ENTER.

Highlight 'Racer X: The Article that Inspired the Movie' and press the RIGHT arrow on your remote to reveal a yellow steering wheel.

Press ENTER to view one of the movie's car stunts from different angles.

★ ★ ★ ★

2) Action Featurette

Select 'Special Features' from the Main Menu and press ENTER.

Highlight 'Racer X: The Article that Inspired the Movie' and press ENTER.

The article appears onscreen. Press the UP arrow on your remote to reveal a yellow steering wheel at the top of the screen.

Press ENTER for a short clip featuring interviews with Vin Diesel, Paul Walker and director Rob Cohen.

★ ★ ★

Father Ted: The Complete 1st, 2nd and 3rd Series (Box Set)

A warm and brilliantly farcical sitcom that ran for just three years and twenty-four episodes, *Father Ted* introduced us to three mad Irish priests and their equally bonkers housekeeper, who preach the word of God (or attempt to) on tiny, desolate Craggy Island.

There's Father Ted Crilly, of course, marvellously played by Dermot Morgan as the one trying to hold all the insanity together, the dim-witted but well-meaning Father Dougal McGuire (Ardal O'Hanlon) and foul-mouthed, booze-sodden Father Jack Hackett (Frank Kelly), whose vocabulary is almost entirely limited to the words 'Feck', 'Drink', 'Arse' and 'Girls'.

With Pauline McLynn's Mrs Doyle on hand to make the tea and add to Ted's calamitous adventures, this is a perfectly formed home-grown comedy, skilfully scripted by Graham Linehan and Arthur Mathews.

Easter Egg

Character Highlights

Insert Disc 4 (Third Series), select 'Extras' from the Main Menu and press ENTER.

Highlight 'Dougal's Album' and then press the UP arrow on your remote to highlight the photo frame.

You can now choose to see clips of Dougal, Ted , Jack or Mrs Doyle by choosing their photos and pressing ENTER.

There is also a photo of a horse. Select this and you see the 'My Lovely Horse' video.

★ ★ ★ ★

Fawlty Towers: The Complete Series 1 & 2 (3-Disc Set)

John Cleese's comic creation remains a classic, perhaps in part because only twelve episodes of *Fawlty Towers* were ever made, making sure the show – unlike many other situation comedies – never had the chance to go stale. Originally, however, no one predicted its enduring success when it first aired on BBC2 in 1975: the first series only garnered three million viewers (which in the days when we had only three TV channels to choose from wasn't very impressive).

But word of mouth grew and the show set in a fictional Torquay hotel became a favourite, thanks to Cleese's manic portrayal of hotel owner from hell Basil Fawlty, Prunella Scales' Sybil and, of course, Andrew Sachs' incompetent Spanish waiter/dogsbody/whipping boy Manuel.

The DVD includes all twelve thirty-minute episodes (including, of course, the much-loved one with the Germans), plus an extra disc of interviews with John Cleese, Prunella Scales and Andrew Sachs, out-takes and a short documentary.

Easter Egg

Fawlty Towers: The Location

Insert Disc 3 (extras disc).

The 'Special Features' menu will appear – highlight 'Guest Registry'.

Press the RIGHT arrow on your remote. This will highlight the main photo on the right.

Press ENTER to see a video of the building that was used for the exterior shots of the hotel.

The Fifth Element

Director Luc Besson's stylish (costumes by Jean Paul Gaultier, no less) science-fiction adventure has Bruce Willis being both muscly and sensitive as Korben Dallas, a former government agent turned cab-driver in twenty-third-century New York who has a strange girl named Leeloo (Milla Jovovich) literally fall into his lap from a great height. So begins an imaginative, unusual adventure mixing comedy with action as Korben, Leeloo and monk Cornelius (Ian Holm) attempt to save the universe from destruction and the machinations of the evil Zorg (Gary Oldman).

The leads – especially Oldman, who overplays it all with tongue-in-cheek gusto – look like they are having tremendous fun, but most impressive are the jaw-dropping sets, from the futuristic New York scenery to the impressively realised resort of Fhlotson Paradise.

Sadly, the DVD isn't exactly brimming over with extras (cast and crew biographies are just about it), but with so much packed into the film itself, it's hard to quibble.

Easter Eggs

1) Hidden Sketches And Trailer

On the Main Menu, highlight 'Subtitles'.

Press the UP arrow on your remote to highlight the large 'The Fifth Element' logo.

Press ENTER.

A drawing of the movie's ship will appear.

From this page, press the LEFT arrow for a picture of Zorg's (Gary Oldman) pet from the movie.

From this page, press the RIGHT arrow for a picture of the movie's futuristic city.

From this page, press the UP arrow for a photo of the diva.

On this page, press the DOWN arrow and the teaser trailer for *The Fifth Element* will start.

★ ★ ★

2) Milla Jovovich Interview

On some versions of *The Fifth Element* DVD, there is a 'Gallery' option in the Main Menu.

Select the 'Gallery' and press ENTER.

On the Gallery menu, select the 'Four Elements' feature and press ENTER.

Proceed to the second page, where you will find the words 'It Must Be Found'.

Use the UP arrow on your remote to highlight the word 'Must'.

Press ENTER and the 'S' in 'Must' will have changed colour. Press ENTER again until the 'S' turns red. Press ENTER once more and the 'S' bursts into flames. MTV's interview with Milla Jovovich in Cannes will now play.

Final Destination 2

Final Destination, if you remember, was the deliciously vindictive horror film about a teenager who has a premonition that the plane he and his pals are about to board will crash. While the group misses the flight (which does indeed go down), death nevertheless then catches up with them one by one. (If you never saw the first movie, you can still understand the second as a newscaster at the beginning here helpfully explains the events of part one.)

This sequel follows a similar pattern. This time a young woman named Kimberley (A. J. Cook) survives a freeway pile-up (a year to the day after the aforementioned plane crash) and rescues other people from the wreckage, only to see them soon dropping like flies, usually in the most gruesome of circumstances.

It's typical horror hokum, of course, but there's some twisted fun to be had in guessing who will next meet their grisly death, and in exactly which nasty fashion they will expire.

Easter Egg

Hidden Clips

Select 'Beyond the Movie' from the Main Menu and press ENTER.

Press the LEFT arrow followed by the DOWN arrow on your remote.

Lightning will appear in the microwave. Press ENTER.

This opens almost fifteen minutes of hidden clips, including screen tests and behind-the-scenes footage.

Final Fantasy: The Spirits Within

A computer-animated science-fiction adventure based on a video game, *Final Fantasy* was greatly anticipated by Hollywood studio executives who hoped the 'digital actors' (photo-realistic, digitally animated characters) would allow them finally to fire all those expensive, pesky human actors and replace them with more pliable animation.

While the lead female character, Aki, did get her own photo feature in a men's magazine, it doesn't look like Julia Roberts, George Clooney and Tom Cruise need to sign on for the dole just yet. The animation is superb (the 'actors' even have flaws, such as stubble and spots) but the plot is predictable (something about saving the planet from evil phantoms), the dialogue clichéd and the characters paper-thin (although there is some nice vocal acting from Alec Baldwin, Donald Sutherland, James Woods, Steve Buscemi and *ER*'s Ming-Na as Aki).

The DVD features a 'making of' documentary, deleted scenes, storyboards and commentaries.

Easter Eggs

1) Thriller
Insert Disc 2 (bonus disc), select 'Highlights Menu' from the Main Menu and press ENTER.

Select the right symbol of the two at the bottom and press ENTER to go to the second page of highlights.

Highlight the 'up triangle' at the bottom of the page and then press the RIGHT arrow twice on your remote to highlight the box on the right.

Press ENTER for the animated characters from the movie performing their own version of Michael Jackson's 'Thriller' video.

★ ★ ★ ★

2) Storyboard

On Disc 2, highlight 'Highlights Menu' on the Main Menu.

Press the RIGHT arrow on your remote, followed by the DOWN arrow twice to reveal a symbol.

Press ENTER to view the storyboards of a romantic dinner for character Aki.

★ ★ ★

3) Lighting Test

On Disc 2, highlight 'Play Documentary' on the Main Menu.

Press the LEFT arrow followed by the UP arrow on your remote to reveal an Oriental symbol.

Press ENTER for a 3-D lighting test on Aki's face.

4) Concept Sketches

On Disc 2, select 'Highlights Menu' from the Main Menu and press ENTER.

Select 'Character Files' and press ENTER.

Press the DOWN arrow on your remote, followed by the RIGHT arrow and then the LEFT arrow to reveal a symbol.

Press ENTER for some early sketches.

There are further sketches if you go to the second page of Highlights, select 'DVD Rom Content' and press ENTER.

Press the UP arrow on your remote, followed by the RIGHT arrow, to reveal a symbol, and press ENTER.

★ ★ ★

5) Ships

On Disc 2, select 'Highlights Menu' from the Main Menu and press ENTER.

Select 'Vehicle Scale Comparisons' and press ENTER.

Press the DOWN arrow on your remote, followed by the RIGHT arrow twice to reveal a symbol.

Press ENTER for 3-D drawings and models of the ships.

★ ★ ★

A Fish Called Wanda (2-Disc Special Edition)

Kevin Kline won an Oscar for his hilarious performance as lothario thug Otto in this 1988 comic crime caper packed with funny set-pieces as four criminals try to double cross one another in their attempts to get their hands on the loot from an armed robbery. John Cleese is the barrister who gets caught up in the chaos, Jamie Lee Curtis the moll he falls for, and best of all is Michael Palin as the stammering hitman with a love of animals whose attempts to murder a little old lady lead him to rub out her pet pooches.

The *Python* influence is strong here, of course (Cleese co-wrote the script with director Charles Crichton), and surrealism combines with fabulously bad taste (literally, as Kline scoffs the contents of Palin's fishtank, including the title character) for the movie's best moments. It's just a shame that the four principals had to spoil it all almost a decade later by reuniting for the risible *Fierce Creatures*.

Easter Egg

Hidden Menu

Insert Disc 2, highlight 'Special Features' on the Main Menu and then press the LEFT arrow on your remote.

This reveals a large blue fish. Press ENTER.

You should now see a hidden menu featuring: Jamie Lee

Curtis's Halloween Memento: an out-take from Jamie's interview for the DVD.

The Key to Wanda's Heart: a deleted scene from the movie.

John Cleese's Thoughts on the USA: an out-take from the movie.

Futurama: Seasons 2, 3 and 4 (Box Sets)

Matt Groening's follow-up to the phenomenon that was and is *The Simpsons* may not have shared its success (it ran for only four seasons) but it does have the same sly humour, bright animation and surrealism (and is also deliciously ruder than the more family-friendly Simpson clan).

In 1999, pizza delivery-boy Fry accidentally falls into a cryogenic machine and is frozen for a thousand years, waking at the end of the thirtieth century. Things are quite different in the future – many former US presidents are still active in politics, even though they are now just heads in glass jars, for example – but with the help of an ageing professor (who is also one of Fry's descendants), a foul-mouthed robot named Bender (his catchphrase is 'bite my shiny metal ass') and one-eyed ship's captain Leela, he begins to adapt to his new, but often bizarrely similar, surroundings.

There are a couple of minor Easter eggs in the first-series box set, but the main finds (as listed below) are from seasons 2, 3 and 4.

Easter Eggs
Season 2
1) High School Photos
Insert Disc 1, select the episode 'I Second that Emotion' and press ENTER.

Press the DOWN arrow on your remote until you highlight Nibbler's third eye.

Press ENTER for a high-school-yearbook photo of creator Matt Groening.

On Disc 2, select the episode 'Lesser of Two Evils' and press ENTER.

Press the LEFT arrow on your remote to highlight the crown and press ENTER for a photo of David X. Cohen.

On Disc 3, select the episode 'How Hermes Requisitioned His Groove Back' and press ENTER.

Highlight 'Scene Selection' and then press the UP arrow on your remote to highlight a disk.

Press ENTER for a school photo of writer Bill Odenkirk.

Also on Disc 3, select the episode 'The Problem with Popplers' and press ENTER.

Highlight 'Play' and then press the UP arrow on your remote to highlight the poppler. Press ENTER for a photo of Patric Verrone.

On Disc 4, select the episode 'War Is the H-Word' and press ENTER.

Press the DOWN arrow on your remote until you highlight the remote-control Bender. Press ENTER for a photo of Eric Horsted.

★ ★

Season 3

1) Hidden Intro Captions

On Disc 1, select the episode 'Amazon Women in the Mood' and press ENTER.

Press the LEFT arrow to highlight the computer screen and press ENTER.

A series of unused captions, like those seen at the start of each episode, unroll, including 'Contents Have Been Known to Control the Minds of Livestock' and 'Lick Screen for "Surprise"'.

2) Season's Greetings

On Disc 1, select the episode 'A Tale of Two Santas' and press ENTER.

Press the RIGHT arrow to highlight the TV screen and then press the UP arrow to reveal a Santa hat.

Press ENTER for a Christmas greeting from David X. Cohen in which he insults most of his colleagues.

3) Episode Reading

On Disc 1, select the episode 'A Tale of Two Santas' and press ENTER.

Press the RIGHT arrow to highlight the TV screen and press ENTER. You will be treated to the audio-table read of the episode.

★ ★ ★

Season 4

1) *Star Trek* Clips

On Disc 3, select the episode 'Where No Fan Has Gone Before'.

Highlight 'Home' and press the RIGHT arrow on your remote. The main photo will change to the *Planet Express* ship (with *Star Trek* add-ons).

Press ENTER for two clips from the writer of the episode about writing for *Star Trek* actors. This is followed by John DiMaggio explaining the origins of Bender's voice.

★ ★ ★

2) Alien Message

On Disc 4, highlight 'The Devil's Hands Are Idle Playthings' and then press the LEFT arrow on your remote to highlight an item in the fridge.

Press ENTER for a page of text in the alien language.

(Note: apparently regular, keen-eyed viewers should be able to decipher the language.)

★ ★

3) Episode Reading

On Disc 4, select 'The Devil's Hands Are Idle Playthings' and press ENTER.

Press the UP arrow on your remote to reveal the Devil's Hands.

Press ENTER for an audio-table reading of the episode.

4) Hidden Intro Captions

On Disc 4, select the episode 'Spanish Fry' and press ENTER.

Highlight 'Scene Selections' and then press the LEFT arrow on your remote.

The picture on the computer screen will now have changed to one of Leela, Fry and Bender.

Press ENTER for a series of unused captions, like those seen at the start of each episode, including 'The Flickering Light at the End of the Comedy Tunnel'.

★ ★ ★ ★

The Gift

A creepy, old-fashioned chiller, *The Gift* features a classy cast (Cate Blanchett, Keanu Reeves, Hilary Swank, Katie Holmes, Greg Kinnear), an interesting screenplay co-written by Billy Bob Thornton, and taut, restrained direction from Sam Raimi (best known, of course, for the *Evil Dead* movies and, later, *Spider-Man*).

Widowed mother Annie (Blanchett) makes her living in a small Southern town through psychic readings, but she falls foul of local thug Donnie (Reeves, a revelation here), who is none too pleased that his wife (Swank) listens to her predictions. When a local woman goes missing, Annie has a vision of her dead body that leads to Donnie's arrest. But is he guilty?

While the plot is rather predictable (and regular thriller watchers will figure out the twist before Annie does), the film features terrific performances from a cast that also includes Giovanni Ribisi and Gary Cole, and Raimi keeps the tension mounting until the final showdown.

Easter Egg

The Gift Premiere

Highlight 'Play Movie' on the Main Menu.

Press the LEFT arrow on your remote to reveal a star at the top-left of the screen.

Press ENTER for a series of clips from the movie's LA

premiere, featuring chats with stars Giovanni Ribisi, Keanu Reeves, Cate Blanchett and Hilary Swank, and director Sam Raimi.

Gladiator

After losing forty pounds and building up his muscles to play the role, Russell Crowe won an Oscar and became the thinking woman's crumpet following his role as Maximus, the Roman general turned gladiator in Ridley Scott's deservedly award-winning epic.

Hollywood's first real Roman epic in over thirty years, *Gladiator* follows Maximus' exile from Rome and the murder of his family by Commodus (a seething Joaquin Phoenix), his training as a gladiator, and his quest for revenge. Beautifully made, the film is epic in size and imagery as ancient Rome is recreated perfectly for the screen and captured dazzlingly by cinematographer John Mathieson. As well as the computer wizardry, however, there is a gripping human story of betrayal and revenge, grisly battle sequences, heroic deeds and skilled performances from Crowe, Phoenix, Richard Harris, Djimon Hounsou and Oliver Reed, who sadly died during filming (his remaining scenes were filmed using a stand-in and computer imagery).

The DVD includes commentaries, 'making of' featurettes and galleries of the production.

Easter Eggs

1) The Rhino

On Disc 2, go to the arrow at the bottom of the Main Menu page and press ENTER to access page 2 of the menu.

Select 'Original Storyboards' and press ENTER.

Select 'More' to go to the second page of 'Storyboards'.

Select the 'Rhino Fight' and press ENTER.

Press the UP arrow on your remote to highlight the rhino in the middle drawing.

Press ENTER to reveal a secret menu where you can read the script pages that would have featured the rhino in the gladiator arena, and also view a short CGI test for the rhino that was ultimately deemed too costly to film.

★ ★ ★ ★

2) Region 1 Trailer

If you have a Region 1 version of *Gladiator*, insert Disc 2 and go to the second page of the Main Menu (as above).

Select 'Trailers and TV Spots' and press ENTER.

Press the LEFT arrow on your remote and you will highlight an amulet around Richard Harris' neck.

Press ENTER for a cleverly done trailer for the comedy *Chicken Run* that was produced in the style of the *Gladiator* trailer.

★ ★ ★

The Godfather Trilogy (4-Disc Box Set)

This box set contains two of the most unforgettable films of the 1970s, Francis Ford Coppola's 1972 epic of an Italian-American family *The Godfather*, and its sequel, 1974's *The Godfather Part II*. Also, unfortunately, 1990's huge disappointment, *The Godfather Part III*, is included.

The saga, of course, of the Corleone family, *The Godfather* – based on Mario Puzo's bestselling novel – introduced us to a Mafia family led by Don Vito Corleone (Marlon Brando) at the time when his young son Michael (Al Pacino) becomes involved in the family business, alongside explosive brother Sonny (James Caan).

The characters are all now part of movie history. Lawyer Tom Hagen (Robert Duvall), Michael's second wife Kay (Diane Keaton), sister Connie (Talia Shire), unfortunate brother Fredo (John Cazale) are introduced in the first film, while in *Part II* we see the young Vito (as played by Robert De Niro) rise from Italian immigrant to leader of a major crime syndicate.

Michael's first hit, the horse's head in the bed, and the gunning down at the toll booth are just a few of the scenes that have deservedly become movie legend, but it is in the intricate depiction of the characters' lives that the first two films truly shine. A beautifully realised saga (the first two movies, at least) that remains a testament to a one-of-a-kind director and his skilled cast.

Easter Eggs

1) Mario Puzo

Insert the fourth, 'Extra Features' disc, go to the 'Filmmakers' page and select 'Mario Puzo'.

Press ENTER to see his biography.

Press the LEFT arrow on your remote to reveal a dollar sign ($) on the page.

Press ENTER to hear a five-second clip from Puzo on why he wrote *The Godfather*.

2) Foreign-Language Moments

Select the 'Set Up Menu' on Disc 4 and press ENTER.

This gives you the 'Subtitle Menu'.

Press the RIGHT arrow on your remote and a globe will appear.

Press ENTER to view a minute-long collection of dubbed clips of the movies.

★ ★ ★

3) *The Sopranos*

On Disc 4, select 'Galleries' from the Main Menu and press ENTER.

Select 'DVD Credits' and press ENTER.

Go to the final page by using the NEXT button on each page.

At the end, there is a clip from the TV series *The Sopranos* in which Tony Soprano and his gang attempt to watch a bootleg copy of *The Godfather* and debate their favourite scenes.

★ ★ ★ ★ ★

4) James Caan

On Disc 4, select 'Family Tree' from the Main Menu and press ENTER.

Select 'Sonny' and press ENTER.

Select 'Sonny' again and you will see his biography.

Press the LEFT arrow on your remote to highlight the picture of James Caan and press ENTER.

This reveals James Caan's biography. Press the LEFT arrow to highlight the portrait of him and press ENTER.

This reveals a brief clip, as part of James Caan's original screen test, in which he does a pretty impressive impersonation of Marlon Brando.

Hannibal

After the phenomenal success of *The Silence of the Lambs* (and critical acclaim for the earlier *Manhunter*, also based on a Thomas Harris novel that featured the character Hannibal Lecter), there were high hopes for a sequel, especially as the director taking the helm was visual genius Ridley Scott.

Unfortunately, *Hannibal* didn't meet expectations – mainly because Harris' novel, on which the film is based, was disappointing and implausible (this perhaps explains why *Silence*'s star, Jodie Foster, and director, Jonathan Demme, declined the offer to return for the sequel). Picking up some time after Lecter's (Anthony Hopkins') escape from maximum security at the end of *The Silence of the Lambs*, we find the cannibal enjoying the flavours of Italy (human and otherwise). Meanwhile, FBI agent Clarice Starling (now played by Julianne Moore) meets with Hannibal's only surviving victim, the disfigured Mason Verger (an unrecognisable Gary Oldman), who is almost as twisted as Hannibal in his quest for revenge.

While Moore and Oldman give solid performances, poor Ray Liotta (as Paul Krendler) gets saddled with the worst of the dialogue (but the most memorable scene, in which Hannibal literally has him for dinner), and Hopkins – laying on the menacing looks and lip-smacking moments with a trowel – seems to have turned up only to draw his cheque. The main problem is that Hannibal just isn't quite as menacing uncaged, wandering about like a tourist, and, though Ridley Scott keeps things looking stylish and moving at a fair pace, in the end this is more an interesting footnote than a fulfilling end to the Lecter tale.

Easter Egg

Clarice

Insert Disc 2, select 'Breaking the Silence: The Making of Hannibal Featurettes' and press ENTER.

Highlight 'Music (14.16)' and then press the LEFT arrow on your remote to highlight the two arrows pointing upwards to the left-hand side of the screen.

Press ENTER for a series of flashframes (the pieces of film exposed from the moment the director says, 'Cut!' to the time the camera is turned off) all featuring Julianne Moore, set to the song 'Clarice', written by *Hannibal* music editor Mark Streitenfeld.

★ ★ ★ ★

Harry Potter and the Philosopher's Stone (2 Discs)

Director Chris Columbus – who inflicted Macaulay Culkin in *Home Alone* on the cinema-going public, but over a decade later should probably finally be forgiven for it – was the man burdened with the task of translating the most popular children's book in recent history to the big screen. Fans of trainee wizard Harry weren't disappointed by Columbus' lengthy (two and a half hours) but faithful adaptation of J. K. Rowling's first book, as the director wisely packed as much of the widely read story into the script as was possible. He also had the assistance of a cast that's a *Who's Who* of British acting talent, including Maggie Smith, Alan Rickman, Richard Harris, Fiona Shaw, John Cleese, Ian Hart and Julie Walters.

As everyone who hasn't been living under a rock for the past few years knows, Harry (Daniel Radcliffe) is a young orphan who discovers he's a wizard and is whisked off to Hogwarts School of Witchcraft and Wizardry, where he befriends Ron (Rupert Grint) and Hermione (Emma Watson). The school is run by the wise Professor Dumbledore (Harris), one of the wizards who knows what happened to Harry's parents and why the boy himself may be in danger.

The younger members of the cast may not be the greatest actors in the universe, but they all have their own charms and fit nicely into their roles. Columbus, meanwhile, uses just the right amount of CGI effects to realise this magical world, from the detailed Quidditch match to Hogwarts itself.

The two-disc DVD features a host of extras, including a tour of Hogwarts, games and a visit to Diagon Alley (which you have to complete to gain a wand that allows access to the classrooms and some other areas of Hogwarts, as shown below).

Easter Eggs

1) Cut Scenes

Insert Disc 2 and select 'Diagon Alley' from the Main Menu, then press ENTER.

You have to select the bricks in a clockwise direction. When you get to the last brick before the arrow, press ENTER and you should be allowed in.

Highlight the 'Gringotts' sign and press the DOWN arrow on your remote to highlight the key on the sign. Press ENTER.

You are now inside Gringotts, and since you highlighted the key, you are given money which you need for the next step.

Select 'Ollivanders' and press ENTER.

Choose your wand (hint: it's on the left) and once you have it, leave the shop.

On the Main Menu, select 'Classrooms' in the centre and press ENTER.

Highlight 'Transfiguration' and then press the DOWN arrow on your remote to highlight the owls under the flame.

Press the UP arrow to highlight the 'H'. Press ENTER.

There are now a few quizzes for the younger viewers to get you to the clips, so don't read on if you want to figure it out for yourself:

At Fluffy, select the flute and press ENTER.

At the Keys, select the small one in the middle and press ENTER.

At the Bottles, select the yellow, round bottle and press ENTER.

Select the red stone in the mirror and press ENTER for seven cut scenes, including Harry and Hagrid on the London Underground.

★ ★ ★ ★ (if you have the patience – or a small child – to go through all the steps beforehand).

2) Tasting Beans

Enter Gringotts Bank as above.

At the bottom of the left-hand lamp, highlight the bag of beans and press ENTER.

You can now select beans from the photo and hear how they taste by pressing ENTER.

★ ★

3) Secrets On The Tour

On Disc 2, select 'Tour' and press ENTER.

During the tour, you enter the Gryffindor common room.

The tour stops at a painting and you are given the option of right or left. Press either to turn around until you are given three options (up, in addition to right and left).

Press the DOWN arrow on your remote to highlight something on the wall and press ENTER to see a painting of Quidditch.

You will also go to the Library.

When you are facing the teacher's table and up close to it,

three arrows (up, right, left) appear on the screen. Press the DOWN arrow on your remote and you will highlight something in the left-hand corner.

Press ENTER and you will see the House Cup Scoreboard.

4) Hogwarts Letter

Insert Disc 1 and at the Main Menu, highlight 'Play Movie' and then press the RIGHT arrow on your remote to highlight Hedwig the Owl.

Press ENTER for Harry's letter of acceptance to Hogwarts.

★ ★ ★

The Hitchhiker's Guide to the Galaxy

Originally an innovative 1970s radio show, *The Hitchhiker's Guide to the Galaxy* became an equally ground-breaking TV programme when it was first broadcast by the BBC in 1981.

Based on an idea by Douglas Adams (and later spun off into a series of books, T-shirts, games and the like), the story begins with a bang as Arthur Dent (Simon Jones) is told by his friend Ford Prefect (David Dixon) that the Earth is about to be destroyed to make way for a hyperspace bypass. Prefect, it transpires, is actually an alien spending time on Earth to research a new edition of *The Hitchhiker's Guide to the Galaxy*, and he convinces Dent to catch a lift on a passing Vogon spacecraft so they can both avoid the impending disaster.

That, of course, is just the beginning of their adventures, which are packed with strange creatures, novel language and bizarre moments. All the episodes of the cult series are contained on the DVD, alongside deleted scenes, out-takes and a photo gallery.

Easter Eggs

1) Pan-Galactic Gargle Blasters

Insert Disc 1. On the Main Menu, highlight 'Set Up' and then press the LEFT arrow on your remote.

This reveals a keypad asking you to enter a code.

Highlight 1 and press ENTER, then 1 and ENTER, then 4 and ENTER and finally 6 and press ENTER – you will have entered 1146 (the time the Earth was destroyed).

You will now see the complete sequence showing the destruction of the Earth, followed by an advertisement for Pan-Galactic Gargle Blasters.

★ ★ ★

2) Infected DVD

On Disc 1, select 'Play All' from the Main Menu and press ENTER.

After about fifteen seconds, press TITLE on your remote (this will return you to the Main Menu).

As soon as the music finishes on the Main Menu, press ENTER.

The first episode will start, but the titles will move around the screen and the audio will go fast and slow. Then a message will appear telling you your DVD has been infected by the Infinite Improbability Drive.

This can be a tricky one to get to work, but is worth the effort.

★ ★ ★ ★

3) Computer Displays

Insert Disc 2, select 'Outer Planets' from the Main Menu and press ENTER.

On the 'Outer Planets' menu, select 'Subtitles On' and press ENTER.

Highlight 'The Inner Planets' and then press the LEFT arrow on your remote to reveal a 'Don't Panic' logo.

Press ENTER to see a series of computer displays from the series.

★ ★

4) Opening Credits

On Disc 2, select 'Subtitles Off' on the Main Menu (the 'Inner Planets' menu) and press ENTER.

Highlight 'Communicate' and then press the LEFT arrow on your remote to reveal a picture of the Earth.

Press ENTER to see the full opening titles from *Hitchhiker's Guide*.

★ ★ ★

I'm Alan Partridge
(Series One and Two)

Steve Coogan and Armando Iannucci's comic creation, the Pringle-jumper wearing, banality-spouting radio and TV presenter (as played by Coogan) who could have been based on any number of Radio 2 DJs, first came to our screens as the sports reporter on *The Day Today*, before returning in 1994's spoof chat show, *Knowing Me, Knowing You*.

This follow-up, beginning three years later, has the ageing, bitter Alan – not exactly flavour of the month with TV bosses any more, especially as his chat show ended with a guest being shot – making a living of sorts on Radio Norwich. He lives at the local Travel Tavern just off the M11, takes out his frustrations on his PA Lynn and has numerous future TV projects turned down by short-sighted executives.

Superbly scripted by Coogan, Iannucci and Peter Baynham, and featuring great performances from Coogan, Felicity Montagu (as Lynn) and Phil Cornwell (as Dave), this is one of the best TV comedies of recent years. The DVDs for both series include deleted scenes and out-takes, commentaries and biographies on the cast and crew.

Easter Eggs

Series One

BBC Logo

Insert Disc 2, press the RIGHT arrow on your remote until the menu option 'Optionalan' appears.

Press ENTER.

Highlight 'Subtitles Off' and then press the UP followed by the LEFT arrow on your remote.

The word 'TWAT' appears on the wall behind Alan.

Press ENTER for a clip of the BBC logo, and Alan and Lynn talking about it.

★ ★ ★

Series Two
Hidden Clip

Insert Disc 2, select 'Anglian Alan' from the Main Menu and press ENTER.

Select 'Credits' and press ENTER.

Select 'Executive Producer Alan Partridge' and press ENTER.

Go to the second page of Alan's biography by selecting the arrow at the bottom of the page and pressing ENTER.

Highlight the arrow at the bottom of the page and then press the UP arrow on your remote to reveal a helicopter symbol in the middle of the text.

Press ENTER for a clip of Alan's 'Crash Bang Wallop What a Video'.

★ ★ ★

Independence Day (2-Disc Special Edition)

Yes, this sci-fi action adventure has some cheesy dialogue (especially during Bill Pullman's climactic patriotic speech) but Dean Devlin and Roland Emmerich's blockbuster is also hugely entertaining, thanks to tongue-in-cheek performances from the cast and lots of flashy effects.

Jeff Goldblum is the computer whizz who hears a satellite transmission that could be coming from outer space (and may not be friendly), so he rushes off to tell the President of the United States (Pullman) that a visit from ETs may be imminent.

While Will Smith, Randy Quaid, Robert Loggia, Pullman and Goldblum all give terrifically fun turns, the special effects – from the alien ships that arrive to hover over major cities (a pretty blatant rip-off of the TV series *V*, it has to be said) to the explosions as they obliterate landmarks such as the Empire State Building and the White House – steal the show. Not exactly brain-straining fare, but a great popcorn movie nevertheless.

Easter Egg

Hidden Menu

Insert Disc 2, select 'Data Console' from the Main Menu and press ENTER.

Highlight 'Main Menu' and then press the RIGHT arrow on your remote.

A red light will come on to the hard disk of the computer onscreen. Press ENTER.

The ship in the background will start to hover and 'ACCESS 7-4-ENTER' appears on the computer's monitor. This is the access code you need to enter the ship.

Return to the Main Menu, press 7, then 4, then ENTER on your remote. This allows you to enter the alien ship and see the hidden menu.

The menu includes 'Combat Review', in which you can view the various scenes of alien destruction on Earth, and 'Monitor Earth Broadcasts', a collection of the news clips featured in the film.

★ ★ ★ ★

Insomnia

Just when we thought Robin Williams was going to spend the rest of his movie career boring us with sentimental dross like *Patch Adams* and *Bicentennial Man*, he surprised everyone by turning in superb – and somewhat creepy – performances in *One Hour Photo* and the gripping *Insomnia*, in which he ably shares the screen with one of Hollywood's best actors, Al Pacino.

Pacino is Detective Will Dormer, a cop sent to Alaska to investigate the murder of a teenage girl. While finding a suspect is easy – local author Walter Finch (Williams) has a connection to the dead girl – Dormer is soon caught up in a web of blackmail and deceit. His investigation is further complicated by the twenty-four-hour-a-day sunlight that stops him sleeping.

Directed by Christopher Nolan, who made *Memento* with Guy Pearce, and based on a cracking 1997 Norwegian film, this is gripping fare that benefits from a taut script, atmospheric direction and striking Alaskan and Canadian scenery, as well as two stunning central performances that are not to be missed.

The DVD features commentaries from co-star Hilary Swank and director Nolan, among others, trailers and featurettes about the making of the film.

Easter Egg

Secret Footage

Select 'Bonus Materials' from the Main Menu and press ENTER.

Select 'Production Diaries' and press ENTER.

Highlight 'Bonus Material' at the bottom of the screen and press the LEFT arrow on your remote. One of the pencils on the floor in the picture should be highlighted.

Press ENTER for footage shot by director of photography Wally Pfister of an avalanche that occurred during shooting of the film as director Christopher Nolan and star Hilary Swank look on.

Jerry Maguire (2-Disc Collector's Edition)

Writer/director Cameron Crowe gave Tom Cruise one of the best roles of his career so far in this drama that also showcased the talents of Renée Zellweger five years before *Bridget Jones's Diary*.

Jerry Maguire (Cruise) is a top wheeling-and-dealing sports agent at a big agency until the day he sees the light and writes a 'mission statement' – a heartfelt memo to his bosses telling them it's the people they represent, not the money they make, that count.

Of course, none of his superiors agree with this foolish notion, and Jerry is fired, left to start again with just one client, erratic footballer Rod Tidwell (Cuba Gooding Jr, in an Oscar-winning performance) and an assistant in the form of young single mother Dorothy (Zellweger).

Cruise is charming as the agent at a loss in his personal and professional lives, and he is ably supported by Zellweger, Gooding Jr, Bonnie Hunt (as Dorothy's sceptical sister) and the almost-too-cute Jonathan Lipnicki (as Dorothy's six-year-old son). A successful blend of comedy, drama and romance, this also has the cool soundtrack (Springsteen, The Replacements, Tom Petty) that has become a trademark of Crowe's films.

Easter Egg

Unseen Commentary Footage

Insert Disc 2, select 'Special Features' from the Main Menu and press ENTER.

Select 'Director and Cast Video Commentary' and press ENTER.

Highlight 'Mission Statement' and then press the RIGHT arrow on your remote and press ENTER. (You should hear the background music pause.)

Highlight 'Mission Statement' again and then press the RIGHT arrow on your remote, followed by the UP arrow. This should highlight letters on the keyboard.

Press ENTER for some behind-the-scenes footage of Cameron Crowe, Cuba Gooding Jr, Renée Zellweger and Tom Cruise preparing to film the DVD video commentary.

★ ★ ★ ★

Lara Croft: Tomb Raider

After the disasters that were *Mortal Kombat*, *Streetfighter* and *Super Mario Bros*, it's surprising that anyone was willing to hand over the cash to make another movie based on a video game. *Tomb Raider*, of course, had the advantage that the central character was a sexy female archaeologist rather than a squat Italian plumber or an expressionless chopsocky fighter, but there was still a risk that the hordes of pimply boys locked in their basements playing with computer consoles wouldn't venture out to the cinema to see a live-action version of their favourite heroine.

In the end, though, the first of Lara's cinematic adventures was a hit, despite a flimsy plot and uninspired direction from Simon West. Its success is largely due to the casting of Angelina Jolie (complete with posh British accent) as Lara, the titled woman who spends her time in a snug all-in-one Lycra ensemble scrabbling for ancient artefacts. There's also good support from Angelina's real-life dad Jon Voight (as Lara's father), Daniel Craig, Iain Glen and *Shine*'s Noah Taylor – their performances almost make up for the fact that they are appearing in an Indiana Jones rip-off (without any remotely scary bad guys).

Easter Egg

Angelina Jolie And Jon Voight

Select 'Special Features' from the Main Menu and press ENTER.

Highlight 'Main Menu' and then press the DOWN arrow on your remote to highlight a wave symbol.

Press ENTER to reveal a clip featuring Angelina Jolie and Jon Voight talking about acting together in the film.

The League of Gentlemen (Series One and Two and Christmas Special)

British comedy at it's most bizarre, *The League of Gentlemen* is so strange, twisted and macabre that it makes *Twin Peaks* look like an episode of *Crossroads*. Obsessively adored by fans, and treated with puzzlement by those who don't get its pitch-black and quirky humour, it's set in the fictional town of Royston Vasey and features such odd characters as serial killers Edward and Tubbs, the local shop-owners with a dislike for strangers, butcher Hilary Briss, vet Matthew Chinery (who 'accidentally' slaughters animals in his care) and Barbara Dixon, the local cab-driver who's halfway through a male-to-female sex change.

Based on a stage show that rose to prominence at the Edinburgh Fringe Festival, *The League of Gentlemen* is written by Mark Gatiss, Steve Pemberton, Reece Shearsmith (who all star in the series) and Jeremy Dyson. The Christmas Special, like the two series, pays homage to Gothic comedy and seventies horror movies, and looks at different aspects of life in Royston Vasey (town motto: 'You'll Never Leave').

Easter Eggs

Series One
Audio Clips

On the first menu, answer the question 'Are You Local?' by selecting 'Yes' and then press ENTER. (If you answer 'No' the screen goes blank – remember, Royston Vasey residents don't like strangers.)

Select 'Precious Things' from the Main Menu and press ENTER.

Select 'Local People' and press ENTER.

Select 'The Denton Family' and press ENTER.

Highlight 'Local People' and then press the LEFT arrow on your remote to hear an audio clip. This should work for all the characters (however, you have to return to the 'Local People' Main Menu after hearing a clip, and then select a new character from there).

★ ★

Series Two
Extra Footage

Insert Disc 2, highlight 'Missing' from the Main Menu and then press the LEFT arrow on your remote.

This takes you to a screen asking you to type in an 'easy number to remember'.

The phone number you need is for Pop's flat (444 4244) – highlight each number and then press ENTER (as you go, the numbers will appear at the bottom of the screen).

Press ENTER for some behind-the-scenes footage of the crew from the series.

★ ★ ★

Christmas Special

1) Hampstead House Of Horrors

Select 'Stocking Fillers' from the Main Menu and press ENTER.

Highlight 'Tales from Beyond the Crypt' and then press the LEFT arrow on your remote.

This reveals a Christmas wreath. Press ENTER.

You are taken to a game of Hangman and asked for a password. The password is 'prawn toast'.

Once you have spelled out that, you will be shown the League's early film *Hampstead House of Horrors*.

★ ★ ★ ★

2) Line Dancing

Select 'Audio Set-up' from the Main Menu and press ENTER.

While the Audio menu is on screen, you will hear dialogue and then the choir begins singing. At this point, 'RIP' will appear below the cherub in the centre in the screen.

Highlight 'RIP' and press ENTER.

This takes you to a scene showing Charlie's line dance which you can watch from three angles.

★ ★ ★

The Lord of the Rings: The Fellowship of the Ring and the Two Towers (Special Extended DVD Editions)

Peter Jackson's trilogy, based on J. R. R. Tolkien's classic novels, is one of the most ambitious productions in movie history, a skilful mix of superb performances, stunning scenery and magical computer-generated imagery to suit the unforgettable story.

A tale of hobbits, elves, dwarves and other creatures who populate Middle Earth, the first two parts of the trilogy are available on DVD in special extended versions, both featuring well over half an hour of extra footage (*The Two Towers* features a whopping extra 43 minutes of scenes, making it a bladder-straining 223 minutes in total) to expand further on the adventures of hobbits Frodo (Elijah Wood) and Sam (Sean Astin) as they attempt to destroy an evil ring in the fiery depths of Mordor. Helping them in their quest are the 'Fellow-ship': fellow hobbits Merry and Pippin (Dominic Monaghan and Billy Boyd), elf Legolas (Orlando Bloom), warrior Aragorn (Viggo Mortensen), dwarf Gimli (John Rhys Davies) and wizard Gandalf (Ian McKellen).

As well as commentaries from many of the cast (including Christopher Lee, Astin, Wood, Andy Serkis and Miranda Otto) for each film, there are fascinating contributions from director Jackson, plus two discs of documentaries, location guides, behind-the-scenes footage and storyboards for both films. Hardly surprising, then, that there aren't many Easter eggs, since so much fascinating extra stuff has been included already.

Easter Eggs

The Fellowship of the Ring

1) Hidden Trailer

On the second disc (part two of the movie), select the Main Menu and press ENTER.

At the Main Menu, select 'Select a Scene' and press ENTER.

Select chapter '48' and press ENTER.

Highlight 'Official Fan Club Credits' on the resulting page and press the DOWN arrow on your remote.

This reveals a *Two Towers* logo in the lower right-hand corner. Press ENTER.

Director Peter Jackson congratulates you on finding the Easter egg and introduces the original *Two Towers* trailer that was shown in cinemas following the release of *The Fellowship of the Ring*.

★ ★ ★

2) Non-UK Easter Egg

If you have a Region 1, Region 4, or a non-UK Region 2 disc, you can access a terrific *Lord of the Rings* spoof from the MTV

Movie Awards. (It was not included on the UK disc as apparently it was deemed too rude for the film's PG rating.)

On the first disc, select 'Select a Scene' from the Main Menu and press ENTER.

Select chapter '25–27' and press ENTER.

Highlight scene '27' and press the DOWN arrow on your remote. This reveals a ring. Press ENTER for the hilarious MTV spoof starring Sarah Michelle Gellar and Jack Black.

The Two Towers

Non-UK Easter Egg

Bah humbug. Once again, a clip from the MTV Awards isn't included on the UK DVD, but is available on the Region 1 version (and Region 2 versions that are not from the UK).

On the first disc, select 'Select a Scene' from the Main Menu and press ENTER.

Select chapter '29–30' and press ENTER.

Highlight scene '30' and press the DOWN arrow on your remote. This reveals a ring. Press ENTER for Gollum/Andy Serkis' terrific (and occasionally explicit) acceptance speech from the MTV Movie Awards – it's so good, it's almost worth buying a Region 1 player just so you can see it.

★ ★ ★

Magnolia (2-Disc Edition)

Boogie Nights' writer/director Paul Thomas Anderson delivers a twisting, emotional, multiple-plot drama with *Magnolia*, which follows several characters' lives over the course of a day in California. There's a misogynistic sex guru/motivational speaker played by Tom Cruise (even if the film wasn't any good, it would be worth watching just to hear him say, 'Respect the cock'), a quiz-show host with a secret (Philip Baker Hall), a dying man (Jason Robards) and his young wife (Julianne Moore) and a big-hearted cop (John C. Reilly), all of whose lives are connected in some way. These connections, and the coincidences that link them, form the heart of the film.

An ambitious epic in terms of its intricate structure (and its three-hour running time), *Magnolia* addresses big themes such as the true meaning of life, but also focuses on the minutiae of people's everyday existence as we watch these characters slowly fall apart. A film about pain, redemption, forgiveness, love and family, there are superb performances and a memorable song, 'Wise Up' by Aimee Mann, that is hauntingly performed.

Easter Egg

Out-takes

Insert Disc 2, select 'Colour Bars' from the Main Menu and press ENTER.

A colour-bar test card will appear on the screen.

Wait approximately twenty seconds and you will see a collection of out-takes from the film.

★ ★ ★ ★

The Matrix and The Matrix Revisited

Possibly the best movie Keanu Reeves has made (although *Speed* scores points for sheer fun), *The Matrix* is a clever, riveting sci-fi blockbuster, featuring jaw-droppingly amazing special effects (including the now famous and much imitated 'bullet time') and smart ideas that put George Lucas' *Star Wars* prequel *The Phantom Menace* (released the same summer) to shame.

As the film's millions of fans know, Reeves is Neo, a computer hacker who is trying to contact the mysterious Morpheus (Laurence Fishburne) just as the latter contacts him, to tell our hero-of-sorts that there's a group of sinister-looking men, led by Agent Smith (Hugo Weaving) after him. It turns out that what Neo thinks is reality really isn't, and the Earth he knows as home may be nothing more than a façade created by the evil cyber-intelligence known as the Matrix. And, of course, Morpheus and his rebels are convinced that Neo is their only hope in their struggle against the all-seeing, impossible-to-escape Matrix, which is sapping the life from humans who are completely unaware of their mind-boggling predicament.

Smartly written and directed by the Wachowski Brothers, this is packed with stylishly leather-clad good guys (including the skin-tight number sported by co-star Carrie-Anne Moss) and creepy, shadowy baddies. Slick, sexy and very, very cool, *The Matrix* injected new life into the sci-fi genre, mixing philosophical ideas with beautifully choreographed action sequences and breathtaking visuals. (Shame the movie's two sequels *Matrix: Reloaded* and *Matrix: Revolutions* weren't as narratively inventive).

The Easter eggs below are for the DVD of the first movie in the trilogy and for the *Matrix Revisited*, a stand-alone extras DVD that can be bought separately or as part of a 2-disc *Matrix* set.

Easter Eggs

The Matrix

1) Bullet Time

Select 'Special Features' from the Main Menu and press ENTER.

Select 'The Dream World' and press ENTER.

Highlight the red pill below the 'Follow the White Rabbit' option by pressing the DOWN arrow on your remote. (Yes, this is possibly the simplest egg to find . . . ever.)

Press ENTER for a short documentary explaining 'What Is Bullet Time?'

★ ★ ★ ★

2) The Concept

Select 'Special Features' from the Main Menu and press ENTER.

Select 'Cast and Crew' and press ENTER.

Select 'Written and Directed by the Wachowski Brothers' and press ENTER.

Highlight the red pill on the page by pressing the DOWN arrow on your remote.

Press ENTER for clips, concept sketches and CGI work under the title 'What Is Concept?'

★ ★ ★ ★

The Matrix Revisited

1) Girl In Red

Select 'Go Further' from the Main Menu and press ENTER.

Highlight 'What Is To Come' and press the RIGHT arrow on your remote to reveal the Girl in Red in the main picture.

Press ENTER for a short clip about filming the scene featuring the Girl in Red.

2) Hugo Weaving

Select 'Go Further' from the Main Menu and press ENTER.

Highlight 'What Is To Come' and press the RIGHT arrow on your remote to reveal the Girl in Red in the main picture.

Press the RIGHT arrow again to reveal Agent Smith in her place.

Press ENTER for a clip about Hugo Weaving's injury during filming.

★ ★ ★ ★

3) Jukebox

Select 'Languages' from the Main Menu and press ENTER.

Highlight 'English' in the subtitles menu and then press the LEFT arrow on your remote to reveal a phone.

Press ENTER to enter the hidden Juke Box, featuring a selection of forty-one songs you can play.

★ ★ ★ ★

4) Hidden Trailer

Select 'Languages' from the Main Menu and press ENTER.

Highlight 'English' in the subtitles menu and then press the LEFT arrow on your remote to reveal a phone.

Press ENTER to enter the hidden Juke Box.

On the first page of music, select 'Continue' and press ENTER to go to tracks 11–20. Press the RIGHT arrow on your remote to reveal the bullets onscreen around Keanu Reeves and press ENTER to see a trailer for *The Matrix*.

★ ★ ★

5) Keanu Reeves

Select 'Go Further' from the Main Menu and press ENTER.

Select 'Continue' and press ENTER to go to the second page.

Highlight 'The True Followers' and then press the RIGHT arrow on your remote (Keanu Reeves will strike a pose).

Press ENTER for a series of behind-the-scenes clips featuring Keanu Reeves.

★ ★ ★ ★

Me, Myself & Irene

In 2000 Jim Carrey reunited with the Farrelly Brothers, who had directed him in *Dumb and Dumber*, for this less successful comedy.

Carrey plays Charlie, a mild-mannered Rhode Island cop who falls in love with Irene (Renée Zellweger). That would be fine except Charlie has another personality, Hank, lurking beneath the surface, who is everything Charlie is not – violent, angry and rude are just some of his qualities – and, of course, he's very interested in Irene, too.

Unfortunately, that's about it for plot. The majority of the movie is left empty of anything like a story, leaving the way clear for Carrey to take over the screen with his two personas, sweet Charlie and offensive, manic Hank. Even Zellweger doesn't get much of a look-in as the bad taste (but intermittently funny) moments are piled on thick and fast. A disappointment following the Farrellys' *There's Something About Mary*, but one that will raise a few (guilty) laughs.

Easter Eggs

1) Charlie And Hank Menus

On the Main Menu, highlight 'Language Selection' and then press the RIGHT arrow on your remote to highlight the pill on screen. Press ENTER.

A message will appear saying it is time for Charlie to take his medicine. If you select 'Thanks, I Almost Forgot', you will be returned to the Main Menu.

If you select 'No Thanks, I Feel Fine' and press ENTER, you will get a different Main Menu, featuring Hank.

★ ★ ★

2) Out-takes

On the Main Menu, select 'Chapter Selection' and press ENTER.

Select chapters '13–15' and press ENTER.

Highlight chapter '14' and then press the DOWN arrow on your remote to reveal a green Jim Carrey head.

Press ENTER for a short series of out-takes from the movie.

★ ★ ★ ★

Memento

A clever, mesmerising modern film noir from director Christopher Nolan, *Memento* tells a story in reverse chronological order, then moves forward, revealing pieces of a fascinating puzzle as it goes.

It has a murder-mystery tale at its centre: Leonard (Guy Pearce) is seeking to avenge the rape and murder of his wife. The problem is that he suffers from a rare form of amnesia that makes it impossible for him to make new memories, so each morning he wakes up unable to remember the events of the day before (or any day in the past few months, for that matter), and unable to judge just who are his friends and who could be the possible killer. His only aids are the Polaroids and notes that he makes, and the important messages he has tattooed on his body to help him in his quest.

An irritating gimmick in another director's hands, *Memento*'s backwards and forwards storytelling is brilliantly delivered by Nolan, while the cast – including Joe Pantoliano and Carrie-Anne Moss – never let anything slip before its time.

The DVD features the shooting script, commentaries, a tattoo gallery, interviews and biographies.

Easter Egg

'The Beginning Of The End'

Many copies of this DVD have a sticker on them saying 'Hidden

Feature: "The Beginning of the End"' so you know the Easter egg is included.

Select 'Special Features' from the Main Menu and press ENTER.

The various special features appear as Polaroids spiralling across the screen.

As the words of the final one, 'Memento mori', disappear from view, press ENTER.

(This is a matter of timing, so you may have to try more than once to access it, but luckily the special features repeat if you miss it first time.)

A title screen will appear telling you that you have found the hidden feature, which is a re-edited version of the movie, in chronological order.

If you press ENTER you can watch the whole movie, from the end to the beginning (beginning with the credits running backwards). Fascinating to watch after first seeing the movie the way it was intended.

★ ★ ★ ★ ★

Men in Black II (2-Disc Special Edition)

The Men in Black are back to save the universe once more in this second adventure from director Barry Sonnenfeld starring Will Smith and Tommy Lee Jones.

As fans of the movies well know, there are aliens living incognito among us on Earth, and the MiB is the secret government agency who police them, wiping people's memories if necessary so we never find out what is really going on.

This time around, Agent K (Jones) has 'retired' from the MiB and works in a post office, unaware of his previous life. But when Agent J (Smith) needs his pal's help, he restores K's memory so the pair can fight the evil Serleena, a Kylothian monster cunningly disguised as a lingerie model (Lara Flynn Boyle).

The plot isn't up to much, but all the sci-fi comedy ideas that made the first film a huge hit are here: the great teaming of Smith and Jones, Frank, the talking pug, Rip Torn as the man in charge, the funny script ('Silly little planet. Anyone could take over the place with the right set of mammary glands') and the bonkers special effects (including a giant, angry worm).

The DVD includes trailers, a Barry Sonnenfeld commentary, featurettes and a blooper reel.

Easter Egg

Training Video

On Disc 1's Main Menu, highlight 'Scenes' and then press the UP arrow on your remote to reveal the words 'MiB Training Video' next to the alien.

Press ENTER for the MiB training video, which features appearances by 'celebrities', including Vernon Kay, Caprice and, scariest of all, Richard Madeley.

★ ★ ★ ★

Monsters Inc. (2-Disc Collector's Edition)

The animation whizzes at Pixar – the studio that gave us the *Toy Story* movies and *A Bug's Life* – delivered another feast for the eyes with this funny tale of a couple of cuddly monsters.

As kids have always known, there really, truly, are monsters hiding in our closets ready to scare us when the lights go out. What we didn't know is that there is a monster town named Monstropolis on the other side of those wardrobe doors, and the residents cross over into the human world to give small children a fright because our screams power all their gadgets and gizmos.

Mike (voiced by Billy Crystal) and Sully (John Goodman) work at Monsters Inc. (big blue beast Sully is the best at getting screams from humans; Mike is his planet-shaped assistant). Sully accidentally allows a cute kid to follow him back into the monsters' world, causing chaos (monsters are afraid of human children, you see) and sending them on a fast-paced adventure.

Like Pixar's previous movies, the computer animation is a treat, the script witty for adults and kids, and the actors voicing the characters perfectly cast, with Steve Buscemi and James Coburn ably supporting Crystal and Goodman. The DVD is packed with extras, from a tour of Pixar's studios to witty 'out-takes' from the film, and a handful of Pixar shorts, as well as the eggs below.

Easter Eggs

1) Air Show

On Disc 2, select the 'Humans' World' door and press ENTER.

Now select the 'Pixar' door and press ENTER.

Highlight the Monsters Inc. logo in the right-hand corner and then press the LEFT arrow on your remote to reveal a circle showing the paper aeroplane's flight path.

Press ENTER to see the staff at Pixar having a paper aeroplane air show in their office atrium.

★ ★ ★

2) Hidden Gallery

On Disc 2, select the 'Humans' World' door and press ENTER.

Select the 'Tour' and press ENTER.

At the end of the eighteen-minute tour, a screen filled with doors will appear.

Select the top-left door and press ENTER for a series of sketches from Pixar employees describing how they would utilise the Pixar atrium.

Back at the door page, select the upper-middle door and central door for other short surprises (some fun out-takes that also appear in the out-take extra on the disc and a furry Pixar pal).

★ ★

3) Hidden Trailer

On Disc 2, select the 'Monsters' World' door and press ENTER.

On the menu screen press the RIGHT arrow on your remote to highlight the eye of the Monsters Inc. logo.

Press ENTER to see the very funny Monsters Inc. 'Charades' trailer, which also features on the 'Release' section of the disc.

★ ★ ★

Moulin Rouge! (2 Discs)

Quite simply one of the best and most original musicals ever made – *Moulin Rouge!* is MTV crashing head on with nineteenth-century Paris as realised by writer/director Baz Luhrmann.

A mad assault on the senses, the film stars Ewan McGregor as Christian, an impoverished writer in Paris who falls in love with the beautiful star of the Moulin Rouge, Satine (Nicole Kidman). Of course, their love can never have a happy ending, as Satine is promised to the flesh-crawlingly sinister Duke (Richard Roxburgh), and, unbeknown to Christian, she is also suffering from consumption (didn't her discreet coughs and pale complexion tip him off?).

Only in this strange, spectacular place – where absinthe flows freely, and bohemians, members of the aristocracy, dancers, singers, scantily clad chanteuses and even Toulouse Lautrec (John Leguizamo) enjoy the decadent party – would you expect to hear Jim Broadbent (as the Moulin Rouge's owner) serenading the Duke with a version of Madonna's 'Like a Virgin', or the assembled dancers performing a mournful but sexy version of the Police's 'Roxanne'.

Luscious and inventive, the film is packed with eye-widening set-pieces and enjoyable performances, while the DVD features an impressive collection of extras, including a commentary from Luhrmann, 'making of' featurettes, extra scenes, galleries and biographies, as well as a record-breaking *fifteen* Easter eggs. What more could you possibly ask for?

Easter Eggs

1) John Leguizamo

Insert Disc 2 and select 'The Stars' from the Main Menu. Press ENTER.

When 'The Stars' menu appears, highlight 'More' and press ENTER.

Highlight 'John Leguizamo' and press the UP arrow on your remote to reveal a green fairy.

Press ENTER to see a clip of Leguizamo dressed up in a sitar-shaped costume.

2) Ewan Farewell

On Disc 2, select 'The Stars' from the Main Menu. Press ENTER.

Type '9' and press ENTER, then type '17' and press ENTER.

This reveals a lovely clip of Baz Luhrmann saying farewell to Ewan McGregor with a special surprise.

★ ★ ★ ★

3) Ewan and Nicole

On Disc 2, select 'The Cutting Room' from the Main Menu and press ENTER.

Highlight 'Main Menu' at the bottom of the page and then press the LEFT arrow on your remote to reveal a red windmill.

Press ENTER to see a very funny clip of Ewan McGregor and Nicole Kidman performing 'Your Song'.

★ ★ ★ ★

4) Baz Luhrmann

On Disc 2, select 'The Story Is About' from the Main Menu and press ENTER.

Highlight 'Interview with Writers Baz Luhrmann & Craig Pearce' and then press the RIGHT arrow on your remote to reveal a green fairy.

Press ENTER for a clip of Baz Luhrmann trying a visual gag.

★ ★ ★

5) Rehearsal

On Disc 2, select 'More' at the bottom of the Main Menu and press ENTER to go to the second menu page.

Select 'The Dance' and press ENTER.

From the next menu, select 'The Dance' and press ENTER.

Highlight 'A Word From Baz' and press the RIGHT arrow on your remote to highlight a green fairy.

Press ENTER for Baz talking to the dancers.

★ ★

6) Baz Dances

Select 'The Dance' from the second Main Menu page as before and press ENTER.

Select 'Choreography' and press ENTER.

Highlight 'Main Menu' and then press the RIGHT arrow on your remote to reveal a red windmill.

Press ENTER to see Baz Luhrmann trying out the choreography.

7) Baz Again

On Disc 2, select 'More' at the bottom of the Main Menu and press ENTER to go to the second menu page.

Select 'The Music' and press ENTER.

Select 'The Lady Marmalade Phenomenon' and press ENTER.

Highlight 'Main Menu' and press the LEFT arrow on your remote to reveal a red windmill.

Press ENTER for a brief clip of Baz Luhrmann in a car.

★

8) More Baz

On Disc 2, select 'More' at the bottom of the Main Menu and press ENTER to go to the second menu page.

Select 'The Design' and press ENTER.

Select 'Set Design' and press ENTER.

Select 'Spectacular Spectacular' and press ENTER.

Scroll through the gallery to the second picture, which has a green fairy highlighted on it.

Press ENTER for a clip of Baz trying to enter the studio.

★

9) Nicole Kidman And Richard Roxburgh

On Disc 2, select 'More' at the bottom of the Main Menu and press ENTER to go to the second menu page.

Select 'The Design' and press ENTER.

Select 'Set Design' and press ENTER.

Select 'The Gothic Tower' and press ENTER.

Scroll through the gallery to the fifth picture which has a red windmill highlighted on it.

Press ENTER for a brief out-take of Nicole Kidman proposi-tioning Richard Roxburgh (who plays the Duke).

★ ★ ★

10) Ewan And Nicole Out-take

On Disc 2, select 'More' at the bottom of the Main Menu and press ENTER to go to the second menu page.

Select 'The Design' and press ENTER.

Select 'Costume Design' and press ENTER.

Select 'A Courtesan's Wardrobe' and press ENTER.

Scroll through the gallery to the fourth picture and there is a green fairy at the top of the screen.

Press ENTER for an out-take in which Ewan McGregor has a little technical problem.

★ ★ ★

11) The Can-Can

On Disc 2, select 'More' at the bottom of the Main Menu and press ENTER to go to the second menu page.

Select 'The Design' and press ENTER.

Select 'Costume Design' and press ENTER.

Select 'The Bohemians' and press ENTER.

Scroll through the gallery to the fifth picture which has a red windmill on it.

Press ENTER for Ewan McGregor, John Leguizamo and other members of the cast trying to dance the can-can.

★ ★ ★

12) Make-up

On Disc 2, select 'More' at the bottom of the Main Menu and press ENTER to go to the second menu page.

Select 'The Design' and press ENTER.

Type '18', then press ENTER. (You may hear your DVD player reacting.) Then press '99' and ENTER for a clip of the make-up artist dusting nipples. It's not quite what you expect . . .

★ ★ ★

13) Top Hats

On Disc 2, select 'More' at the bottom of the Main Menu and press ENTER to go to the second menu page.

Select 'The Design' and press ENTER.

Select 'Smoke and Mirrors' and press ENTER.

Type '5' and then ENTER. Then press '18' and ENTER for a clip of how they got the top hats to fly into the air.

★ ★ ★

14) Costume Test

On Disc 2, select 'More' at the bottom of the Main Menu and press ENTER to go to the second menu page.

Select 'Marketing' and press ENTER.

Select 'Photo Gallery' and press ENTER.

Highlight 'Ellen Von Unwerth' and then press the RIGHT arrow on your remote to reveal a red windmill.

Press ENTER for a short clip of John Leguizamo's costume test.

★ ★

15) Jim Broadbent

On Disc 2, select 'More' at the bottom of the Main Menu and press ENTER to go to the second menu page.

Highlight 'Back' at the bottom of the page.

Press the DOWN arrow on your remote for an out-take with Jim Broadbent strutting his stuff.

The Mummy Returns (2 Discs)

A sequel to the surprise 1999 success *The Mummy*, *The Mummy Returns* stars Brendan Fraser and Rachel Weisz as now-married adventurers Rick and Evelyn, who spend their time wandering through tombs and digging up ancient riches. This time, their young son is kidnapped and Imothep (Arnold Vosloo), the mummy they thought they had disposed of in the first film, is back, stronger and angrier than ever (well, so would you be if people kept resurrecting you when you were having a nice nap).

The plot is implausible, to say the least – especially the stuff about Evelyn possibly being the reincarnation of Nefertiti – but director Stephen Sommers nevertheless delivers a rip-roaring adventure in the Indiana Jones vein, but with extra twenty-first-century bangs, whistles and special effects, plus, of course, the enjoyable addition of wrestler The Rock as the powerful Scorpion King.

The two-disc DVD set includes numerous extras, including background information on ancient Egypt and the history of mummies.

Easter Egg

Mummification
Insert Disc 2, select 'Bonus Materials' and press ENTER.

Select 'Egyptology 201' and press ENTER.

Select 'An in Depth Look at Mummification' and press ENTER.

Press the RIGHT arrow on your remote twice to highlight the scorpion.

Press ENTER for a short featurette about modern-day mummification.

★ ★ ★

Not Another Teen Movie

A spoof teen movie (erm, wasn't *Scary Movie* and its sequels doing this already?), this broad comedy sends up moments from films like *Cruel Intentions*, *Varsity Blues* and *She's All That* (and, in case we didn't get the joke, the school here is John Hughes High School – duh).

All the stereotypes are present and correct – the token black guy, the popular jock and even the foreign girl who spends most of the movie semi-naked – but the jokes are curiously lacking (check out the opening vibrator scene – embarrassing, yes, but did you actually laugh?). Still, this did give us the superb Marilyn Manson cover of 'Tainted Love' (and the funny video to match), so it can't be all bad …

Easter Egg

Kiss Out-takes

Select 'Scene Selection' from the Main Menu and press ENTER.

On the first page of scenes, highlight the rubber duck at the bottom and then press the DOWN arrow on your remote.

This reveals a pair of lips on the larger gentleman in the middle.

Press ENTER for a series of out-takes of the lesbian kissing scene from the movie.

★ ★

Ocean's 11 (1960)

Not the remake with George Clooney and Brad Pitt, this *Ocean's 11* is the movie that Frank Sinatra made with his Rat Pack pals – Dean Martin, Sammy Davis Jr, Joey Bishop, Peter Lawford and honorary member Angie Dickinson.

All Quiet on the Western Front director Lewis Milestone was the man trying to rein in the chaos of these five guys let loose in Las Vegas, who, along with six wartime pals, decide to rob five casinos in just one night (the five venues – the Flamingo, Riviera, Sands, Desert Inn and Sahara – were all places where Frank, Sammy and Dean had performed in real life).

It was all really just an excuse for Frank and his gang to have a good time while filming (pal Shirley MacLaine pops up in an unbilled cameo as a drunk woman, which she later said she filmed just so she could hang out with the boys for a few days), and the plot does take second place to their drinking, womanising and cool rapport. A true slice of the early sixties.

Easter Egg

Las Vegas Gambling Museum

Select 'Special Features' from the Main Menu and press ENTER.

Highlight 'Cast and Crew' and then press the LEFT arrow on your remote.

This should highlight one of the gaming chips.

Press ENTER for a short clip about the Casino Legends Hall of Fame in Las Vegas.

★ ★

The Office: The Complete First Series

A stroke of comic genius from creators Ricky Gervais and Stephen Merchant, who met while working at XFM Radio and devised a 'mockumentary' about an office led by the sort of annoying twerp (who thinks he's funny but patently isn't) whom we have all worked for at one time or another.

Set in the fictitious Slough paper merchants Wernham Hogg, *The Office*'s first season was shown in 2001 and introduced us to slimy, inappropriate manager David Brent (the creepily brilliant Gervais in his acting debut), whose mantra is 'I'm a friend first, boss second and entertainer third'; Tim (Martin Freeman), the office dreamer who clearly wishes he was somewhere else; Dawn (Lucy Davis), the receptionist; and wannabe soldier Gareth (the ghoulish-faced Mackenzie Crook).

Made without a laugh track and simply not needing one, it's surely the best British TV comedy of this millennium so far. The DVD includes the entire first season, as well as a second disc of deleted scenes and a documentary.

Easter Eggs

1) Freelove Freeway

Insert Disc 1 and wait for the Main Menu to appear.

Listen to the background office noise and, after a few

minutes, when you hear the phone ring, press ENTER.

You will now see David Brent singing the complete version of 'Freelove Freeway' that appears in Episode Four.

★ ★ ★ ★

2) Peter Purves

Insert Disc 2 and select 'Deleted Scenes' from the Main Menu. Press ENTER.

There is a flickering fluorescent light on the page. Press ENTER as soon as the light begins to fade and you will see the entire training video 'Who Cares Wins', presented by Peter Purves, that is seen briefly in Episode Four.

★ ★ ★ ★

The People Vs Larry Flynt (Collector's Edition)

A film that whipped up a storm of controversy upon its release in the USA, *The People Vs Larry Flynt* is the (mostly) true story of *Hustler* publisher Flynt (Harrelson), the poor Kentucky boy who built up a porn-magazine empire in the seventies and ended up as the unlikely advocate of the First Amendment (the right to free speech) in the Supreme Court. Directed by Miloš Forman and produced by Oliver Stone, the film focuses on Flynt's battles with the US legal system over his explicit mags, his relationship with his bisexual fourth wife, Althea Leasure (Courtney Love), and the flirtation with Christianity which almost destroyed his porn empire.

Harrelson is amusing as Flynt, who was paralysed by a sniper's bullet, but it is Love who is mesmerising as the former stripper who ran Flynt's empire until her AIDS- and heroin-related death. This glossed-up, entertaining version of Flynt's life doesn't concentrate enough on their bizarre but moving relationship, instead chopping back and forth to Flynt's various court cases while attempting to portray him as a champion of the people (not bad for a man who admitted to having sex with chickens as a boy). Ultimately, it's an interesting, but not wholly satisfying, drama.

Easter Eggs

1) Larry Flynt Speaks

Select 'Special Features' from the Main Menu and press ENTER.

Highlight 'Larry Flynt Exposed' and then press the LEFT arrow on your remote to reveal a badge on Woody Harrelson's jacket.

Press ENTER for the real Larry Flynt's presidential campaign ad.

2) More Larry Flynt

Select 'Audio Set Up' from the Main Menu and press ENTER.

Highlight 'French' and then press the RIGHT arrow on your remote to reveal a badge.

Press ENTER for more of Larry's TV campaign.

★ ★ ★

Pirates of the Caribbean: The Curse of the Black Pearl (2-Disc Special Edition)

Who would have thought the best blockbuster of the summer of 2003 would turn out to be one based on a Disney theme-park ride? Or that Johnny Depp, an actor better known for skilled performances in small-scale, critically acclaimed dramas, would be the movie's star?

Certainly, on paper *Pirates* didn't look like a hit. But from the moment Depp appears onscreen as pirate Jack Sparrow, complete with braided hair, black eyeliner and a Keith Richards (Depp's inspiration for the part) accent, it takes all of co-stars Orlando Bloom, Geoffrey Rush and Keira Knightley's skill not to be acted right off the screen.

The story is simple: evil Barbossa (Rush) and his crew, who mutinied against Captain Jack Sparrow and stole his beloved ship, the *Black Pearl*, have kidnapped Elizabeth Swann (Knightley) from her Caribbean home. The local love-lorn swordmaker, Will (Bloom), vows to get her back with the reluctant help of Sparrow, and the pair set off on a swash-buckling adventure packed with sword fights, gallant deeds and witty one-liners. It's like one big pantomime, but that's part of the joy to be had from this hugely entertaining adventure.

The DVD features a shipload of entertaining extras, including commentaries from Depp and director Gore Verbinski, a gag reel, deleted scenes and a documentary about the theme-park ride on which the film is based.

Easter Eggs

1) Time Lapse Construction

Insert Disc 2, go to 'Fly on the Set' and press ENTER.

Place the arrow next to the 'Play All' option and press the RIGHT arrow on your remote twice.

This should highlight one of the monkey's teeth. Press ENTER.

You will now see a two-minute sequence of time-lapse photography showing how the pirate's cave was constructed (yes, you literally see paint dry).

★ ★ ★

2) Computer-Animated Storyboard

On Disc 2, go to the Main Menu, select the 'Below Deck' section and press ENTER.

Place the arrow next to the 'Set Sail' option and press the LEFT arrow on your remote twice.

The skull in the coin should be highlighted. Press ENTER.

This reveals a six-minute computer-animated clip of how the ship chase was planned.

★ ★ ★

3) Keith Richards

On Disc 2, select the 'Moonlight Serenade' section and press ENTER.

Place the arrow next to the 'Main Menu' option and then press the DOWN arrow on your remote twice.

This should highlight the skeleton's tooth. Press ENTER.

There's a brief interview with Keith Richards here, in which he talks about how he felt when Johnny Depp told him he was the influence for the latter's portrayal of Jack Sparrow.

★ ★ ★ ★

4) Foreign Language Trailer

On Disc 2, select 'Below Deck' and press ENTER.

Now select 'Scene Index' and press ENTER.

In the 'Scene Index' menu go to 'NEXT', which takes you to the 'On Deck' menu.

Go to 'Pirate Ships' and then press the LEFT arrow on your remote.

This will highlight a ring on the skeleton hand. Press ENTER to view a foreign-language version of the movie's trailer.

★ ★

Planet of the Apes (2-Disc Special Edition)

With Tim Burton at the helm, this should have been a terrific reworking of the 1968 classic sci-fi film, but sadly, somewhere in the translation, it all went very wrong (apparently even some of the cast members have admitted they are puzzled by the ending).

Mark Wahlberg is sadly miscast as the astronaut in 2029 whose mission goes awry, leaving him stranded on a strange planet where talking apes rule over humans who are treated as slaves. With the help of besotted chimpanzee Ari (Helena Bonham Carter), our hero attempts to evade the gorilla army led by General Thade (Tim Roth, chewing and spitting out the scenery with relish) and uncover the secrets hidden in a remote area called the Forbidden Zone.

While the effects and ape make-up are impressive, this just isn't as much fun as the original, despite some nods in that direction (Charlton Heston, the star of the 1968 version, even has a cameo as Thade's dad, and gets to utter the same line he did first time round: 'Damn them. Damn them all to hell!').

The DVD features commentaries, extended scenes, documentaries and 'enhanced viewing mode' – a feature that allows you behind the scenes as you watch the movie.

Easter Eggs

1) Monkey Commentary

Insert Disc 1 and select 'Special Features' from the Main Menu. Press ENTER.

Select 'Commentaries' and press ENTER.

The Commentary option for Tim Burton should be highlighted. Press the RIGHT arrow on your remote to reveal an ape in the centre of the screen.

Press ENTER for a short clip of the film, narrated by monkeys.

2) Auditions

Insert Disc 1 and select 'Special Features' from the Main Menu. Press ENTER.

Select 'Cast and Crew Profiles' and press ENTER.

Select 'Cast' and press ENTER.

Select 'Estella Warren' and press ENTER.

On her biography page, press the UP arrow on your remote to reveal an arrow next to her photo.

Press ENTER to view an early audition. (This also works for actors Erick Avari and Luke Eberl.)

★ ★ ★

Predator (2-Disc Special Edition)

A classic action/sci-fi film of the 1980s, *Predator* pitted commando Arnold Schwarzenegger and his equally muscular pals (Carl Weathers, Bill Duke and Jesse Ventura) against a mean-looking reptilian alien in the South American jungle.

Tautly directed by John McTiernan (*Die Hard*), this is all about Arnold kicking extraterrestrial butt (not as easy as it sounds, considering the alien in question can render himself invisible) as his squad is picked off one by one (usually in a particularly gruesome fashion).

Not exactly brain-straining stuff, but a terrific example of mindless action and brawn, if you like that sort of thing.

Easter Eggs

1) John McTiernan

Insert Disc 1, select 'Special Features' from the Main Menu and press ENTER.

Highlight 'DVD Rom' and then press the LEFT arrow on your remote to reveal the three dots to the left of the screen.

Press ENTER for a short interview with the movie's director, John McTiernan.

★ ★ ★

2) Stan Winston: Practical Joker

Insert Disc 2, select 'Predator Special FX' from the Main Menu and press ENTER.

Highlight 'Predator (Red) Looking Down' and then press the UP arrow on your remote (three red dots will appear at the bottom of the screen).

Press ENTER for a featurette on Stan Winston, the creature's creator, and the practical joke he played on Arnold Schwarzenegger during filming.

★ ★ ★

3) Jesse Ventura's Ultimate Goal

On Disc 2, select 'Inside the Predator' from the Main Menu and press ENTER.

Highlight 'Classified Action' and then press the UP arrow on your remote to reveal three dots at the top of the screen.

Press ENTER for a clip of ex-wrestler Jesse Ventura talking about his hopes for his career.

★ ★ ★

4) Don't Drink The Water

On Disc 2, select 'Photo Gallery' from the Main Menu and press ENTER.

Navigate to the seventeenth photo and you will see three red dots to the right of the picture.

Press ENTER to see 'Don't Drink the Water', a featurette on the perils of location shooting.

Raging Bull (2-Disc Special Edition)

Robert De Niro gave one of his finest performances, and deservedly won an Oscar, as real-life boxer Jake La Motta, who went from middleweight champ to pudgy, punch-drunk loser (and, later still, bumbling cabaret performer) in this cinematic masterpiece. Intense and uncompromising, the film focuses on the man behind the headlines – La Motta's jealous streak that alienates his wife (Cathy Moriarty) and everyone else around him, his rages and violence – but also brings the boxing ring to life in black-and-white visions of flashbulbs and blood and brutal blows.

It's a fascinating, disturbing and unforgettable look at not just one man but masculinity in general, vividly brought to the screen by director Martin Scorsese and a cast that also includes Joe Pesci, Frank Vincent and Theresa Saldana.

Extras include the original theatrical trailer, a 'making of' documentary and a selection of jokes from Jake La Motta's cabaret act.

Easter Eggs

1) Jake La Motta

Insert Disc 2. When the Main Menu appears, 'The Bronx Bull' should be highlighted.

Press the UP arrow on your remote to highlight the first 'G' in RAGING at the top of the page.

Press ENTER for a photo gallery of Jake La Motta.

2) Fight Footage

On the Main Menu, 'The Bronx Bull' should be highlighted.

Press the UP arrow on your remote to highlight the first 'G' in RAGING at the top of the page.

Press the LEFT arrow on your remote to highlight the second 'G'.

Press ENTER to view footage of a Jake La Motta fight.

Red Dwarf (Series One, Two and Three)

An often hilarious, quirky comedy from the BBC that began in 1988, *Red Dwarf* is the name of a shabby-looking mining ship hurtling through space. All of the crew are dead thanks to a radiation leak, with the exception of soup-machine repairman Dave Lister (Craig Charles), who has been in suspended animation for the three million years since the accident occurred. Now awake, he's not doomed to float through space completely alone, however, as he's joined by the holographic image of his irritating, dead roommate Arnold Rimmer (Chris Barrie), the ship's cat, who has evolved into a more human lifeform (Danny John Jules), Holly, the ship's onboard computer (Norman Lovett, and later Hattie Hayridge), and, eventually, robot Kryten (Robert Llewellyn).

Sharpest in the earlier series, *Red Dwarf* ran for eight seasons. An American version was also planned (a pilot was filmed with *Frasier*'s Jane Leeves as Holly) but never came to light.

Easter Eggs

Series One

1) Polaroid

Insert Disc 2, select 'Bonus Material' and press ENTER.

Highlight 'Deleted Scenes' and then press the UP arrow on

your remote to highlight a photo on the noticeboard.

Press ENTER to watch a Polaroid of Lister developing. (This is one for people with *far* too much time on their hands.)

★

2) Animated Producers

Insert Disc 1, highlight 'Select Episode' on the Main Menu and then press the RIGHT arrow on your remote to highlight the number 4691 on the clipboard. Press ENTER.

You will now see a keypad onscreen – select '4', then press ENTER to highlight the number 4, then '6' (plus ENTER), '9' (plus ENTER), then '1' (plus ENTER).

This will take you to an animated conversation with the producers about the series, and includes them reading out some of their reviews, naming and shaming the reviewers. (Just in case they do another series, I think *Red Dwarf* is wonderful.)

★ ★ ★ ★

Series Two
Animated Producers II

On Disc 1's Main Menu, press the DOWN arrow on your remote twice to highlight the watch. Press ENTER.

At the Holly Hop Box, select 'Start' and press ENTER for an animated discussion with the producers about the episode 'Queeg'.

Series Three

Animated Producers III

On Disc 2, select 'Bonus Material' from the Main Menu and press ENTER.

Select 'Bonus Menu Plain Text' and press ENTER.

Highlight 'Back' and then press the LEFT arrow on your remote to highlight the rabbit (one of the forms of the Polymorph).

Press ENTER to hear the producers talking about the 'Polymorph' episode, again animated.

★ ★ ★ ★

Reservoir Dogs

Much imitated but never bettered, *Reservoir Dogs* was a truly superb debut from writer/director Quentin Tarantino, who was just twenty-eight years old when he wrote the script.

It all centres on a heist, one we join after it has already gone horribly, and bloodily, wrong. The film flashes back so we see how the group of criminals involved are brought together by Joe Cabot (Lawrence Tierney), and given new names so no one knows the others' identities – Mr Brown (Tarantino), Mr Orange (Tim Roth), Mr Pink (Steve Buscemi), Mr White (Harvey Keitel) and Mr Blond (Michael Madsen). And we also learn of the events leading up to the opening scene.

Making this so much more than just a heist movie, of course, are Tarantino's unmistakable, funny and sharp dialogue, clever plotting, and a profusion of memorable scenes, such as the infamous torture sequence featuring Mr Blond, an unfortunate cop, an ear and Stealers Wheel's 'Stuck in the Middle with You' (Tarantino's use of just the right song at just the right time is inspired, too).

A true classic of 1990s cinema, and a remarkable debut from a unique writer/director.

Easter Egg

Quentin Tarantino

Select 'Special Features' from the Main Menu and press ENTER.

Highlight 'Introduction by Quentin Tarantino' and then press the LEFT arrow on your remote. This reveals an ear.

Press ENTER for a hidden twenty-six-minute interview with Quentin Tarantino, in which he talks about the title of the movie and what it means, who the hero of the movie is, the casting, the movie's style and his start in the movie business.

Resident Evil

Yet another movie based on a video game, this is a prequel to the events that happen in the zombie-fighting game (which means there is a smidgen of plot to go along with the copious killing and blood-splattered effects).

Paul Anderson (*Event Horizon*) directs the ghoulish tale with glee as soldier Alice (Milla Jovovich, in regulation clingy outfit, of course) leads a team into a research centre called The Hive, where all the workers have been infected by a virus that has turned them into zombies. If our motley crew of heroes don't complete their mission in time, the world will be infected by the disease, and, to add to her woes, Alice has no memory, so you just know that as soon as she recovers from her amnesia some vital plot point will be revealed that will make matters even worse.

Of course, the story plays second fiddle to the splatterfest (particularly impressive is the damage done to one of the troops by a laser), and the British and American cast wander around the set shooting anything that moves. Not the best zombie movie by a long way, but certainly not the worst adaptation of a video game, either.

Easter Egg

Slipknot Video

(Note – this egg is mentioned on the packaging of the DVD.)

Select 'Set Up' from the Main Menu and press ENTER.

A 'door-locking system' code appears at the bottom of the screen – this is the number you need to access the egg.

Select 'Main Menu' and press ENTER to return to the Main Menu.

Highlight 'Special Features' and then press the LEFT arrow on your remote to reveal a small symbol in the right corner.

Press ENTER. You will now be asked to type in the code you were given. (Use the arrow keys to highlight a number and press ENTER after each digit.)

If you do this within thirty seconds (there is a timer on the screen), you will be taken to the Slipknot 'My Plague' music video.

★ ★ ★

The Ring

A slick Hollywood remake of the 1998 Japanese horror, this has a simple but gripping premise – an unmarked video is being circulated and, if you watch it, you get a phone call saying you will die seven days later (which you do). Unfortunately, reporter Naomi Watts watches the tape's haunting images, and realises she has only a week in which to work out what they mean and also discover how she can stop the video's curse before it's too late.

Fans of the Japanese film (and its sequels and prequel) rightly argue that this is a glossy version that doesn't have the slow-burning atmosphere of the original, but *The Ring* has some truly creepy moments (especially if you are watching it alone), including the startling scene of a horse breaking free on a ferry and the images of a young girl whose story Watts has to investigate to find the true story of the tape.

Easter Egg

Secret Video

On the Main Menu, highlight the 'Look Here' section and then press the DOWN arrow on your remote, followed by ENTER.

You will now see the creepy two-minute video (check out the moving fingers in the box – yuck) that causes all the problems in the movie. And, spookier still, as it returns to the Main Menu, you will hear a phone ringing. Are you scared yet?

★ ★ ★ ★

Robin Williams: Live On Broadway

Robin Williams – who has deservedly won critical acclaim for his more serious acting roles in *Good Will Hunting*, *Insomnia* and *One Hour Photo* (while rightly being criticised for sappy rubbish like *Patch Adams* and *Bicentennial Man*) – returned to his stand-up comedy roots in July 2002 for a one-off gig at the Broadway Theater in New York.

You can almost smell the perspiration as he tears up and down the stage, throwing sharply aimed comic barbs at Tony Blair, George Bush, the Olympics and even his own sex life. The DVD also features an interview with Williams and the extra 'Noises', which is exactly what it sounds like – a compilation of the various sounds Williams makes while onstage (the intentional ones at least).

Easter Egg

X-Rated Robin Williams

(Note – this egg is mentioned on the DVD box.)

Select 'Bonus Features' and press ENTER.

Highlight 'Resume' at the bottom of the screen.

Press the RIGHT arrow on your remote to reveal a 'Parental Advisory Explicit Lyrics' logo.

Press ENTER to hear a two-minute stream of expletives, all the swearing from the show edited together.

 ★ ★ ★

Rocky (Special Edition)

Sylvester Stallone wrote the script (refusing to sell it unless he was cast in the title role), played the lead and presumably made the tea on this 1976 film that later won Oscars for Best Direction (John G. Avildsen), Editing and Best Picture (Stallone was nominated for Best Actor and Best Original Screenplay but lost to Peter Finch in *Network*, and Paddy Chayefsky for that movie's script).

It is, of course, the story of Rocky Balboa (later resurrected in four sequels), a small-time boxer who gets the chance to fight heavyweight champion Apollo Creed (Carl Weathers) for a chance of the top prize (cue inspiring music). A classic rags-to-riches tale of the underdog whom no-one thinks can win, the film mixes Rocky's determined training with a hesitant romance with Adrian (Talia Shire) and the gruff coaching techniques of trainer Mickey (Burgess Meredith).

While it's shocking that *Rocky* pipped *Taxi Driver* to the Best Picture Oscar , it is still a rousing adventure and remained Stallone's best performance until 1997's *Copland*.

Easter Egg

Rocky Meets Stallone

On the Main Menu, press the UP arrow on your remote to reveal the word 'Rocky' in the top left-hand corner.

Press ENTER for a terrific clip in which Sylvester Stallone shows he has a sense of humour (never revealed onscreen, even when he's appeared in supposed comedies) as he meets Rocky.

★ ★ ★ ★

The Rocky Horror Picture Show (2-Disc 25th Anniversary Edition)

It can safely be said that there is no other movie quite like this. Richard O'Brien transferred his cult stage musical to the screen with the aid of director Jim Sharman, and the result is a mad, funny, bizarre and utterly ridiculous adventure that pays homage to B-movies, rock 'n' roll, horror and science fiction.

Young, innocent couple Brad (Barry Bostwick) and Janet (Susan Sarandon) set off to see their former professor on a rainy night, but break down in the middle of nowhere. They decide to take shelter in a nearby mansion, but are unprepared for the people inside – a group of strange characters including Riff Raff (O'Brien), transvestite Dr Frank-N-Furter (Tim Curry), and his creations, Eddie (Meat Loaf) and Rocky (Peter Hinwood).

Packed with classic songs ('The Time Warp', 'Sweet Transvestite' and 'Hot Patootie' among them) and brilliantly bonkers performances, this twenty-fifth-anniversary edition features two versions of the film (accessible from the first disc's Main Menu) – the normal, theatrical version, and an 'audience-participation' version in which viewers are prompted to throw rice, toilet paper, confetti and even toast (though 'buttered' is not recommended), as fans at cinema screenings of the movie have done since it was first released.

The second disc features a deleted scene, documentary, outtakes and trailers.

Easter Egg

Black-and-White Version

On the Main Menu, highlight 'Special Features' and then press the LEFT arrow on your remote.

This reveals a pair of yellow lips.

Press ENTER to go to a *third* version of the movie. In Richard O'Brien's original script, the beginning of the film was to be shot in black and white, only becoming colour when Brad and Janet entered the world of the Transylvanians (as in *The Wizard of Oz*). This version shows what the movie would have been like, beginning in black and white and changing to colour during 'The Time Warp'.

★ ★ ★ ★ ★

Scooby Doo

Exceedingly silly if you're over thirteen years old, but thoroughly enjoyable if you're not, this is a live-action version of the classic Hanna Barbera cartoon, with Sarah Michelle Gellar, Freddie Prinze Jr, Linda Cardinelli and Matthew Lillard as teenagers Daphne, Fred, Velma and Shaggy (Scooby Doo is a CGI creation, voiced by Neil Fanning).

The gang have split acrimoniously, but are reunited when they are all individually invited on a trip to Spooky Island, a resort run by Mondavarious (Rowan Atkinson), where, of course, spooky things are happening, and the mystery is just waiting to be solved.

As in the original cartoons, the most interesting, and funny, moments come whenever Scooby Doo and Shaggy are onscreen (although there are some laughs to be had from Freddie Prinze Jr's awful blond wig), while the rest of the cast are given little to do except look pretty and wait for the inevitable sequel.

Easter Egg

Rainy Season

Select 'Spooky Features' from the Main Menu and press ENTER.

Select the arrow at the bottom of the page and press ENTER to go to the second page of Spooky Features.

Highlight any of the 'Special Features' on the page and then press the LEFT arrow on your remote to highlight the 'Zoinks!' sign.

Press ENTER for a clip about what happens when rain interrupts filming.

★ ★ ★

Shallow Hal

In *There's Something About Mary*, the Farrelly Brothers got laughs from the mentally challenged, so no one should have been shocked when the main joke of this film is Gwyneth Paltrow in a two-hundred-pound fat suit.

But it's actually quite a sweet movie rather than the gross-out comedy we've come to expect from the men behind *Dumb and Dumber*. Jack Black stars as the shallow Hal of the title – a nice enough guy whose big flaw is that he's only attracted to women who are beautiful on the outside. That all changes when Hal gets stuck in a lift with a motivational speaker and emerges unaware that he has been hypnotised into seeing inner beauty. So when he meets and falls in love with larger-than-average, sweet-natured Rosemary (Paltrow) he thinks she's the supermodel type of woman he has always found irresistible.

Surprisingly tame for the Farrellys (although there are a few mildly offensive moments – don't worry), the movie features fun turns from Paltrow (who should do comedy more often, as long as it doesn't turn out like her other foray into the genre, *A View from the Top*), the always watchable Black, and Jason Alexander as his equally blinkered friend, who has a physical 'flaw' of his own.

Easter Egg

The Tail

Select 'Languages' from the Main Menu and press ENTER.

Highlight 'Off' and then press the RIGHT arrow on your remote to reveal a small tail between Jack Black and Jason Alexander.

Press ENTER for a brief clip showing how the 'tail' on Alexander was operated.

The Simpsons: The Complete First Season (Box Set)

Originally a series of short animated clips that were used as fillers in 1987's *The Tracy Ullman Show*, *The Simpsons* as we know it today first hit the screens in 1989, when the unsuspecting world was properly introduced to the yellow family led by Homer and Marge, along with their kids, underachiever Bart, bright spark Lisa and baby Maggie.

A clever mix of fun stories, sharp one-liners, wry observations and movie and television parodies aimed at both adults and children, over the years the series has been criticised for the way it portrays an all-American family (George Bush Sr was particularly offended) and also applauded for the same thing (luminaries such as Paul McCartney, Tony Blair and Elizabeth Taylor certainly all seem to approve, as they have all lent their voices to the show). Whatever the great and the good think, there is no denying that the show is now cemented in the world's popular culture (Homer's catchphrase 'Doh!' even appeared in the *Oxford Dictionary*).

This first-season box set features the early episodes in which Homer's voice is different, and all the characters are a paler shade of yellow, and introduces characters such as Mr Burns and Smithers, Patty and Selma, as well as reminding us how Sideshow Bob's (voice by *Frasier's* Kelsey Grammer) eternal hatred of Bart began.

Easter Eggs

1) Simpsons Magazines

Insert Disc 3, select 'Special Features' from the Main Menu and press ENTER.

Select 'Next' and press ENTER to go to the second page of Special Features.

Select 'Art of the Simpsons' and press ENTER.

Press the LEFT arrow on your remote to highlight Bart's comic.

Press ENTER to see a selection of magazine covers featuring *The Simpsons* from 1989 and 1990.

2) Simpsons T-shirts

On Disc 3, select 'Special Features' from the Main Menu and press ENTER.

Select 'Next' and press ENTER to go to the second page of Special Features.

Highlight 'Some Enchanted Evening Script' and then press the LEFT arrow on your remote to highlight Bart's T-shirt.

Press ENTER to see a short news documentary from 1990 when Bart T-shirts were banned in some schools.

Singin' in the Rain (2-Disc Special Edition)

The film that features perhaps the most famous (and imitated) musical moment of all time, as the wonderful Gene Kelly (who apparently suffered a high temperature on the day of shooting but carried on like a true trouper) dances in the rain, twirling his umbrella to the movie's unforgettable theme song.

Widely regarded as one of the best, if not *the* best, musical of all time, *Singin' in the Rain* was co-directed by Kelly and Stanley Donen and tells the tale of Hollywood's transition from silent movies to talkies as movie-star Don Lockwood (Kelly) has to deal with the fact that his leading lady Lina Lamont (Jean Hagen) has a nails-on-a-blackboard voice that jars with her elegant silent screen image. In steps young ingénue Kathy (Debbie Reynolds) to dub Lina's voice and save the day, as well as provide a love interest for Don.

Packed with memorable moments (in addition to *that* scene, remember Donald O'Connor's 'Make 'Em Laugh' number, and O'Connor and Kelly dancing to 'Moses Supposes'), zippy dialogue and great performances, this is truly a classic musical and a fitting testament to the talents of the late, great Kelly.

Easter Egg

Baz Luhrmann

On Disc 2's Main Menu, press the LEFT arrow on your remote to highlight a wall light by Gene Kelly.

Press ENTER to see *Strictly Ballroom* and *Moulin Rouge!* director Baz Luhrmann talking about *Singin' in the Rain*.

★ ★ ★ ★

Snatch (2 Discs)

British director Guy Ritchie followed his successful debut *Lock Stock and Two Smoking Barrels* with this comedy crime adventure.

Made for a more international audience than the very British *Lock Stock*, *Snatch* features a cast of home-grown favourites (ex-comedian and *EastEnder* Mike Reid, plus *Lock Stock*-ers Jason Statham, Vinnie Jones and Jason Flemyng) alongside Americans Dennis Farina, Benicio Del Toro and, most memorably, Brad Pitt (as the virtually incomprehensible Irish gypsy Mickey).

In spite of the US presence, though, this remains very much a Cockney gangster flick, this time about various hoodlums fighting over a stolen diamond, and there's fun to be had from Ritchie's expletive-packed, fast-paced dialogue and lively action, although not as much as there was in his more memorable debut. (Critics were given further ammunition that Ritchie was a one-trick pony when his next movie, *Swept Away*, a departure from the guns and gags formula, turned out to be an excruciating disaster.)

Easter Eggs

1) Understanding Brad Pitt

On Disc 1's Main Menu, highlight 'Play Movie' and then press the UP arrow on your remote to reveal a speech bubble coming out of the pig's mouth.

Press ENTER and you can choose to have special 'Pikey' sub-titles which appear onscreen whenever Brad Pitt is speaking.

★ ★ ★ ★ ★

2) Snatch Ringtone

On Disc 2's Main Menu, highlight 'Making of Snatch' and then press the UP arrow on your remote twice to reveal a musical note.

Press ENTER for a ringtone like Doug's that you can program into your phone.

★ ★

3) Mike Reid

On Disc 2, highlight 'Making of Snatch' on the Main Menu and then press the UP arrow twice to reveal the musical note.

Press ENTER to go to the ringtone page.

Press the UP arrow on your remote to highlight the photo of Mike Reid and press ENTER for a short, rude message.

★ ★

4) Fines

On Disc 2, highlight 'Making of Snatch' on the Main Menu and then press the UP arrow three times to reveal a dollar sign ('$').

Press ENTER for a list of the fines that were incurred on-set during filming, including £10 for mobile phones ringing, £5 for sleeping on set and £20 for 'whingeing of any nature'.

★ ★ ★

5) Guns And Swearing

On Disc 2, select 'Next' from the Main Menu and press ENTER to go to the second page of 'Special Features'.

Highlight 'B-roll' and then press the UP arrow on your remote twice to reveal an exclamation mark ('!').

Press ENTER and you will reach a page asking you if you are easily offended.

If you answer 'NO', you will get a ninety-second montage of guns and swearing from the movie.

If you answer 'YES', you will get the same clips but with all the swearing bleeped out.

6) Classic Quotes

On Disc 2, select 'Next' from the Main Menu and press ENTER to go to the second page of 'Special Features'.

Highlight 'B-roll' and then press the UP arrow to reveal a '1' for a series of clips from the film featuring memorable dialogue.

Speed (2-Disc Special Edition)

While *The Matrix* may have made him a cult science-fiction star, it was *Speed* that made Keanu Reeves a heart-throb, complete with bulging muscles, smouldering stares and butch bravado.

He stars, of course, as Jack Traven, the hunky cop/bomb-disposal expert/resident beefcake who gets called in when mad bombers are on the loose. And there is no one more barking than extortionist Howard Payne (Dennis Hopper), who has placed a bomb on an LA bus that is set to explode if the bus's speed drops below 50 m.p.h. Luckily there's a feisty gal, Annie (Sandra Bullock), at the wheel to help Jack and his partner (Jeff Daniels) save the day – if they don't run out of freeway first.

It's fast-paced, hi-energy, edge-of-the-seat stuff (think *Die Hard: On a Bus*) from director Jan De Bont that has been much imitated (remember *Speed 2: Cruise Control*, which Keanu wisely passed on?) but never bettered. The two-disc DVD features interviews, documentaries, extended scenes and trailers.

Easter Egg

Passenger Friendly Clip

Insert Disc 2, and on the Main Menu highlight 'Action Sequences', then press the RIGHT arrow on your remote.

This will display a bus picture. Press ENTER.

You may remember that one scene in the movie features the bus crashing into a parked cargo plane at LA airport. This scene was considered a bit much when *Speed* was to be shown as an inflight movie, so it was altered 'to calm the nerves of sensitive passengers', and this clip shows the version that they saw (without the exploding plane!).

★ ★ ★

Spider-Man (2 Discs)

On paper, this looked like a risky prospect: director Sam Raimi, best known for the low-budget *Evil Dead* movies, was somehow at the helm of a big summer blockbuster, with a leading man (Tobey Maguire) better known for sensitive performances in serious dramas like *The Cider House Rules* and *The Ice Storm*. Happily, the end result was, of course, a cleverly realised screen adaptation of the classic Marvel comic, complete with impressive CGI effects, stylish backdrops and fun performances.

To start things off, Raimi draws us into the Spider-Man myth, letting us know just how student Peter Parker (Maguire) went from geeky teenager to brooding superhero after being bitten by a genetically altered spider. Along the way we meet neighbour – and object of Peter's affection – Mary Jane (Kirsten Dunst), Peter's pal Harry (James Franco), Aunt Mae (Rosemary Harris) and Uncle Ben (Cliff Robertson), and Harry's wealthy dad, Norman Osborn (Willem Dafoe), who, like Spidey, cavorts around in a tight lycra outfit, but in his case as bad guy the Green Goblin.

Interestingly, the adventure works best in the dramatic moments rather than the action ones (although some of the Spidey effects rock), as Spider-Man gives Mary Jane an upside-down kiss in the rain, or when the pair meet at a funeral. Maguire and Dunst are perfectly suited to their roles, and while Dafoe's part is underwritten, he clearly has fun as the entrepreneur-turned-psychopath.

There's also much to explore on the two-disc DVD, which includes documentaries, an interview with *Spider-Man* comic creator Stan Lee, screen tests, music videos, commentaries and more.

Easter Eggs

1) Character Files

Insert Disc 1 and select 'Special Features' from the Main Menu. Press ENTER.

Select 'Character Files' and press ENTER.

Then select any of the actors – e.g. Tobey Maguire. Go to the final page of his filmography and press the UP arrow on your remote, which will reveal a circle around his name.

Press ENTER to see a biography on his character (in this case, Peter Parker), with comic-book illustrations. This works for all the main characters – even Aunt May!

★ ★ ★ ★

2) CGI Gag Reel

On Disc 1, select 'Special Features' from the Main Menu and press ENTER.

Select 'Commentaries' and press ENTER.

Highlight the 'Special Features' option at the bottom of the screen and then press the LEFT arrow on your remote.

This will reveal a spider symbol.

Press ENTER for a collection of CGI clips and gags from the making of the film – including Spider-Man and the Green Goblin seemingly doing aerobics together.

★ ★ ★ ★

3) A New Twist On The Webs

Insert Disc 2, select 'The Web of Spider-Man' from the Main Menu and press ENTER.

Select 'DVD-Rom' and press ENTER.

Press the UP arrow on your remote to reveal a mini-spider symbol.

Press ENTER for a short interview with Todd McFarlane in which he explains how he draws Spider-Man's webs.

4) The Romitas

On Disc 2, select 'The Web of Spider-Man' from the Main Menu and press ENTER.

Select 'The Evolution of Spider-Man' and press ENTER.

Move the cursor/Spidey symbol to 'Artists' Gallery' and then press the RIGHT arrow on your remote.

This should reveal the words 'THE ROMITAS' at the top right of your screen. Press ENTER.

This Easter egg is an interview with comic-book artists John Romita and his son, John Jr, who have both illustrated Spider-Man comics.

★ ★ ★ ★

5) Comic-Book Covers

On Disc 2, select 'The Web of Spider-Man' from the Main Menu and press ENTER.

Select 'The Evolution of Spider-Man' and press ENTER.

Select 'Artists' Gallery' and Press ENTER.

Select 'Artists' Gallery' and press ENTER on the following page.

You will now be on a page entitled 'Peter Parker's Darkroom'.

Select 'Comic Book Artist Gallery' and press ENTER.

Select any of the images and press ENTER so it is viewed full screen.

Scroll through the images (each one has an artist credit) until you come to the drawing of Spider-Man by Terry Dodson.

Highlight the camera symbol at the bottom of the screen and press the UP arrow on your remote.

This will reveal Terry Dodson's signature. Press ENTER for a hidden gallery of comic-book cover art.

★ ★ ★

6) The Sinister Six

On Disc 2, select 'The Web of Spider-Man' from the Main Menu and press ENTER.

Select 'The Evolution of Spider-Man' and press ENTER.

Select 'Rogues' Gallery' and press ENTER.

Press the UP arrow on your remote until you highlight the Spider-Man at the top of the page.

Press ENTER to see rotating computer renderings and information on the 'sinister six' – Spider-Man's nemeses from the original comics.

★ ★ ★

7) Full Screen Bad Guys

Go to the 'Rogues' Gallery' as above.

Select Venom, Scorpion or Elektro and press ENTER.

On the subsequent page, highlight the Spidey face at the bottom of the screen and press the DOWN arrow on your remote.

This should reveal a Spider-Man silhouette.

Press ENTER to see a full screen, 3-D computer image of the character.

★ ★ ★

Star Wars: Episode I – The Phantom Menace and Episode II – Attack of the Clones (2-Disc Editions)

Fans of the original *Star Wars* movies (or *Episode IV: A New Hope*, *Episode V: The Empire Strikes Back* and *Episode VI: Return of the Jedi*, to give them their full titles) were understandably disappointed by creator George Lucas' 1999 and 2002 prequels, *The Phantom Menace* and *Attack of the Clones*, both of which were packed with CGI effects but sadly lacking in the wonderment and fun of the first three films.

The Phantom Menace, of course, takes us back to the time when über-evil dude in black Darth Vader was just a small boy named Anakin Skywalker (the teeth-gnashingly annoying Jake Lloyd), eager to be trained in Jedi ways by Qui-Gon Jinn (Liam Neeson) and a pre-Alec Guinness Obi Wan Kenobi (Ewan McGregor).

While the dialogue was worse than an episode of *Crossroads*, and Lucas bogged down the storyline with head-scratching stuff about trade federations and interplanetary politics, there's no denying the backdrops are spectacular, from the magisterial palace on Naboo to the sandswept planet of Tatooine.

Lucas delivered more scenic eye candy in the movie's follow-up, *Attack of the Clones*, and happily we got more action, too, as Anakin became a petulant teenager (Hayden

Christensen) and Obi Wan had his first meeting with bounty hunter Jango Fett (dad of Han Solo's nemesis, Boba). Of course, there was also a terribly naff subplot featuring the blossoming romance between Amidala (Natalie Portman) and Anakin, played against a hilly green backdrop seemingly borrowed from *The Sound of Music*, but Lucas redeemed the trilogy (part three to come in 2005) with the introduction of Christopher Lee's camply evil Count Dooku and a crowd-pleasing display of the power of the force from Yoda (voice supplied by Frank Oz) – the coolest, greenest Jedi of them all.

Both films feature many 'making of' extras and behind-the-scenes looks at how the sets, droids and various creatures were made, which almost – but not quite – makes up for the fact that the movies weren't that great.

Easter Eggs

Episode I – The Phantom Menace

1) Menu Selections

Insert Disc 1. When the UK copyright notice is shown, press 1, 2, 3 or 4 on your DVD remote. (You may also need to press ENTER.)

Each number brings you a different background to the Main Menu when it appears: 1 gives you a simple view of Coruscant; 2 is Tatooine; 3 is Naboo; and 4 is a more intricate view of Coruscant. (These images are randomly selected each time you watch the movie unless you enter one of the four numbers.)

2) Episode I Out-takes

This can be a tricky one to find, so if you can directly access a title on your remote, you should select title '15' after inserting Disc 1 to see the out-takes.

Alternatively, after inserting Disc 1, wait for the Main Menu to appear and then select 'Language Selection' and press ENTER.

At the Language Selection menu, highlight the 'THX' logo in the corner of the screen.

Press 1 1 3 8 on your remote. (On some DVD players you should wait to hear the player react after pressing a number before entering the next. If that doesn't work, try pressing 11, then 3, then 8.) You may need to press ENTER after entering all four numbers, or ENTER after each number.

The out-takes should then appear, and you will be treated to a fun collection of gags – from R2D2 falling over to Yoda (a.k.a. Frank Oz) forgetting his lines.

★ ★ ★ ★

3) Podrace Secrets

Insert Disc 2 and select 'Deleted Scenes and Documentaries', then press ENTER.

On the next menu page, select 'Deleted Scenes Only' and press ENTER.

Now, the menu entry 'Complete Podrace Grid Sequence' should be highlighted.

Press the UP arrow on your remote three times to highlight the 'Doc Menu' entry.

Press the RIGHT arrow on your remote to highlight a small square.

Press ENTER to see a short video clip on the podrace, including a deleted scene featuring Jabba the Hut and his amphibian lunch.

★ ★ ★ ★

4) More Podrace Secrets

There is a second podrace clip. Return to the 'Deleted Scenes' menu (as above).

There are left and right arrows allowing you to navigate between the deleted scenes.

Press RIGHT arrow once and the menu entry 'Extended Podrace Lap Two' will be highlighted.

Press the UP arrow three times, followed by the RIGHT arrow and press ENTER to view a clip about another deleted podrace sequence.

★ ★ ★

5) Two Secrets

These aren't strictly eggs, but they are little extras nevertheless.

On Disc 2, go to the 'Animatics and Still Galleries' menu, where you will get a screen featuring the pit droids sitting on a shop counter. If you wait long enough (about three minutes) without making any selections, Watto comes out and talks to you.

Also, if you go to the 'Trailers and TV Spots' menu, select 'TV Spots' and press ENTER, you will see a screen featuring the Nemoidians. Wait long enough and Darth Sidious will appear.

★ ★ ★

Episode II – Attack of the Clones
1) Menu Selections
When the UK copyright notice is shown on Disc 1, press 1, 2 or 3 on your DVD remote. (You may also need to press ENTER.) Each number brings you a different background to the Main Menu when it appears: 1 is Coruscant; 2 is Kamino; and 3 is Geonosis. (These images are randomly selected each time you watch the movie unless you enter one of the three numbers.)

★ ★ ★

2) Episode 2 Out-takes
If you can directly access a title on your remote, you should select title '15' after inserting Disc 1 to see the out-takes.

Alternatively, after inserting Disc 1, wait for the Main Menu to appear and then select 'Language Selection' and press ENTER.

At the Language Selection menu, highlight the 'THX' logo at the bottom of the screen.

Press 1 1 3 8 on your remote control. (On some DVD players you should wait to hear the player react after pressing a number before entering the next. If that doesn't work, try pressing 11, then 3, then 8.) You may need to press ENTER after entering the four numbers, or ENTER after each number.

Then an out-takes clip will appear, featuring Hayden Christensen fumbling a stunt and, among other fun moments, Ewan McGregor enjoying his ride in a speeder.

★ ★ ★ ★

3) Hidden Gallery

Insert Disc 2, select 'Dex's Kitchen and Stills Galleries' from the Main Menu and press ENTER.

Select 'To Dex's Kitchen' and press ENTER.

Highlight the 'Main Menu' on this page and then press the LEFT arrow on your remote.

This will highlight a square on the wall behind Dex. Press ENTER.

This gives you access to a hidden gallery of *Star Wars Episode II* 'want ads' – a lo-tech college campaign of spoof ads to get students interested in the upcoming movie (look out for Yoda's lonely-hearts ad – it's a gem).

Terminator 2: Judgment Day (2-Disc Ultimate Edition)

1984's *The Terminator* gave Arnold Schwarzenegger the best role of his career (who better to play a monosyllabic, muscle-bound robot?), so it came as no surprise when he reunited with the film's director, James Cameron, for an all-guns-blazing sequel.

Set seven years after Sarah Connor (Linda Hamilton) had defeated the first terminator, the story picks up with Sarah in a mental institution (everyone who hears her story about machines taking over the world in the future understandably thinks she's nuts) and her teenage son John (Edward Furlong), the future leader of the resistance, living with foster parents in LA. That is, until a terminator (Schwarzenegger) is sent from the future to protect John from a more advanced T-1000 cyborg (Robert Patrick) who has been sent back in time to kill him.

Slicker, flashier and faster than the original, this sequel is brimming over with special effects (most notably the ground-breaking morphing of the T-1000), chases and action. Schwarzenegger is terrific as the warmer, fuzzier terminator but the real revelation – in terms of physical brawn, if nothing else – is Hamilton, who buffed up for her role as the tough, bicep-flexing woman who carries on her shoulders the burden of knowing when the end of the world is coming.

Easter Eggs

1) Deleted Scenes

Insert Disc 1. When the Main Menu appears, press 8, then 2, then 9, then 9, then 7 (you will probably have to pause between each number). As you enter the numbers, the words 'The', 'Future', 'Is', 'Not', 'Set' will appear one after the next on the screen.

Press ENTER for two deleted scenes. The first is the T-1000 searching John's bedroom; the second is an alternative, happier ending to the movie.

★ ★ ★ ★

(Note – if you have a Region 1 version of this disc, the number sequence above gives you access to a version of the entire film which incorporates the above scenes.)

2) T-1000

Insert Disc 2. When the 'Cyberdine' logo appears, press the UP arrow on your remote to reveal 'Main Menu'.

This will take you directly to the Main Menu. If you wait without selecting anything for over a minute, a T-1000 will appear and talk to you.

★ ★ ★

They Live

Horror director John Carpenter's 1988 sci-fi thriller about aliens living among us is an enjoyably bonkers yarn, made more so by the deadpan delivery of the film's lead, former wrestler Roddy Piper. He plays an ordinary guy, new to LA, who finds a pair of unusual sunglasses on the street. When he puts them on, they reveal messages like 'Submit To Authority', 'Consume' and 'Obey' on magazine covers and billboards that no one else can see, and also reveal the 'true', alien faces of some of the people around him. It seems the aliens are the rulers of the world, keeping humans in a state of mindless consumerism through these subliminal messages.

This thought-provoking sci-fi premise soon degenerates into an action pic (one fist-fight seems to go on for an age) halfway through, and the film isn't on a par with Carpenter's best work (*Halloween*, *The Thing*), but fans of the genre won't be disappointed. The DVD features commentaries from Piper and Carpenter.

Easter Eggs

1) Mini-Interviews

Select the 'Consume'/'Special Features' menu and press ENTER.

The 'Making Of' should be highlighted.

Press the UP arrow on your remote and the alien's eyes should highlight.

Press ENTER to find the 'Hidden Features' page, which includes profiles of the film's stars, Roddy Piper and Meg Foster, and director John Carpenter.

★ ★ ★

2) Hidden Photo

In the 'Hidden Features' menu (see above), highlight the 'John Carpenter Profile' and then press the LEFT arrow on your remote.

Roddy Piper's sunglasses will be highlighted. Press ENTER to see a photo of Piper and Carpenter in 2002 when they recorded the commentary track for the DVD.

★ ★

Three Kings

Set in the aftermath of the Gulf War, *Three Kings* is a scathingly funny movie from writer/director David O. Russell (*Spanking the Monkey*).

George Clooney, Mark Wahlberg, Ice Cube and Spike Jonze (best known as the director of *Being John Malkovich*) are the disillusioned soldiers who decide to grab the gold bullion hijacked in Kuwait by Saddam Hussein's army and take it for themselves.

Filmed in a reckless, exhilarating style – you don't just see someone shot by a bullet in this movie; you see the bullet entering the body and puncturing an organ – both the motives for the war and the news coverage of it are deliciously exposed, and Russell doesn't flinch from presenting a searing indictment of the brutal madness of armed conflict.

The DVD features a commentary from the director, documentaries and a video diary.

Easter Eggs

1) Hidden Trailer

Select 'Special Features' from the Main Menu and press ENTER.

Select 'Continue' at the bottom of the Special Features page and press ENTER.

Select 'Continue' at the bottom of the second Special Features page and press ENTER.

Highlight 'Theatrical Trailer' and then press the DOWN arrow on your remote to reveal a grenade.

Press ENTER to reveal a sign saying, 'TV SPOT'. Press Enter for a TV trailer.

★ ★ ★

2) Website Passwords

Select 'Special Features' from the Main Menu and press ENTER.

Select 'Cast and Crew' and press ENTER.

Highlight 'Features' at the bottom of the page and then press the UP arrow on your remote to reveal a grenade.

Press ENTER for a secret code that will unlock a part of the Three Kings Events website (details of which are on the DVD-Rom portion of the disc).

The second password can be found by choosing 'Languages' from the Main Menu and pressing ENTER.

On the Languages menu, highlight 'Main Menu' at the bottom of the page and then press the UP arrow on your remote to reveal a grenade.

Press ENTER for the second secret code.

Total Recall

They stole his mind and now poor Arnold Schwarzenegger wants it back in this sci-fi adventure based on a story by Philip K. Dick (also the author of the short story that inspired *Blade Runner*), 'We Can Remember it for You Wholesale'.

Arnie plays Doug Quaid, your average, overly muscled guy of the future, who has recurring dreams about living on Mars. He pays a visit to Rekall, a virtual-reality travel agent, to book a simulated trip to the Red Planet, but when he's hooked up to the machine something goes wrong and Doug awakens from his vacation believing he is some sort of secret agent on a mission. And, since numerous people with guns seem to be after him, maybe he's right.

Director Paul Verhoeven doesn't dwell too long on the familiar Philip K. Dick themes of reality, memories and perception; instead he plunges headlong into lashings of action and violence, beginning when Doug gets his ass kicked by his own wife (Sharon Stone). There's a plotline about the mutants on Mars being exploited, but – while the make-up effects are impressive – it's just a brief diversion from the man with the muscles fighting his way through the spectacular Earth and Mars sets.

Easter Egg

Rekall Advert

Select 'Special Features' from the Main Menu and press ENTER.

Highlight 'Trailer' and then press the LEFT arrow on your remote to reveal a TV symbol.

Press ENTER for the chance to see the full advertisement for virtual vacation company Rekall that was used in the film.

★ ★ ★

Traffic

Loosely based on the 1989 British TV series *Traffik*, director Steven Soderbergh's film exposes various areas of the drug trade in a gritty, documentary style. It focuses on various links in the chain of America's drug culture, from the judge (Michael Douglas) spearheading the President's war against narcotics while encountering drug problems in his own middle-class home to the Mexican cop (Benicio Del Toro, who won an Oscar) using his own questionable methods to get the same job done south of the border.

The cast are all impressive – Don Cheadle and Luis Guzman as DEA agents; Catherine Zeta Jones as a woman whose husband has been arrested for drug crimes; Dennis Quaid, as Zeta Jones's lawyer; and most notably, Erika Christensen as Douglas' heroin-addicted daughter. But most of the plaudits should go to Soderbergh, who embarked on an ambitious project – filming with over 130 actors in 110 locations, mixing film techniques and hand-held camera work – and ultimately delivered a thought-provoking, gritty and powerful piece of cinema.

Easter Egg

Catherine Zeta Jones

Select 'Extra Features' from the Main Menu and press ENTER.

Select 'Production Notes' and press ENTER.

Select 'About the Cast' and press ENTER.

Highlight 'Catherine Zeta Jones' and then press the LEFT arrow on your remote for a fun clip during filming in which Catherine is taken by surprise.

★ ★ ★

Trainspotting (2-Disc Definitive Edition)

Producer Andrew McDonald, writer John Hodge, director Danny Boyle and star Ewan McGregor, the team behind cult hit *Shallow Grave*, reunited for this punchy, occasionally grim look at Edinburgh's drug scene, based on Irvine Welsh's cult novel.

McGregor is Renton, an addict whom we first meet as he runs down the street, spouting the now infamous 'Choose life' speech as he is pursued for committing yet another petty crime to pay for his habit. His life isn't glamorous – hanging out with casual dealer Sick Boy (Jonny Lee Miller), loser Spud (Ewen Bremner) and the psychotic Begbie (Robert Carlyle) – while his drug-addled hallucinations (including his dive into certainly one of the most disgusting toilets in Scotland) are horrific, but when it was first released the film was still criticised by puritanical members of the media for glamorising drug use . In fact, while it never makes any moral judgements about the characters, you would have to be an odd person indeed to find the pointless lives of Renton and his pals even remotely appealing.

Bleakly humorous and brilliantly played (especially by Carlyle, McGregor and Miller), this is simply one of the best British films of the 1990s. The Definitive Edition DVD includes a bonus disc of interviews and interesting extras.

Easter Eggs

1) Critical Comment

Insert Disc 2 (extras disc), select 'Retrospective' from the Main Menu and press ENTER.

Select 'Interviews' and press ENTER.

Select 'Danny Boyle' and press ENTER.

While his interview is playing, after about ten minutes Boyle mentions an article Muriel Gray wrote about the film. When you hear him say her name, press ENTER on your remote to see a collection of newspaper articles (including Gray's for the *Evening Standard*) printed around the time of the movie's release in 1996.

★ ★ ★

2) Porno

On Disc 2, select 'Retrospective' from the Main Menu and press ENTER.

Select 'Interviews' and press ENTER.

Press the RIGHT arrow on your remote to highlight the up arrow at the left-hand side of the screen.

Press the UP arrow on your remote and a short clip of writer John Hodge, producer Andrew MacDonald and director Danny Boyle talking about the possibility of making a sequel to *Trainspotting* (based on Irvine Welsh's novel *Porno*) plays.

★ ★ ★ ★

28 Days Later

A cool, clever zombie movie for the twenty-first century, *28 Days Later* reunited the author of *The Beach*, Alex Garland, with that movie's director, Danny Boyle.

After a group of activists storm a laboratory and free the animals, they inadvertently release a deadly virus that wipes out most of the planet within twenty-eight days. Jim (Cillian Murphy) is one of the few survivors – a scene in which he wanders around the deserted streets of London is breathtakingly creepy – and he soon discovers that many of those who are left are now infected with a rage that turns them into salivating beasts, munching on and infecting anyone they encounter.

Deliciously eerie and terrifically stylish, this is a bloodsplattered treat for fans of the ghoulish, featuring a strong central performance from Murphy and fine support from Brendan Gleeson and Naomie Harris, and Christopher Eccleston as the bonkers army major they encounter.

Easter Egg

Alternative Ending

Select 'Special Features' from the Main Menu and press ENTER.

Select 'Alternate Endings' and press ENTER.

Highlight 'Special Features' at the bottom of this menu and then press the RIGHT arrow on your remote to highlight the small arrow.

This will take you to the Storyboard Alternate Ending.

Press ENTER to see how the movie would have been different if the characters had not encountered the soldiers.

Twin Peaks: The First Season (Box Set)

One of the strangest shows ever to appear on TV, 1990's Twin Peaks was the brainchild of film director David Lynch (*Dune*, *Wild at Heart*) and co-producer Mark Frost (who had previously worked on *Hill Street Blues*). Ostensibly about the investigation into the murder of young Laura Palmer, in fact the show was much more about the secret and strange goings-on hidden beneath the surface of small-town USA, with some sex, violence, betrayal and doughnuts thrown in.

The characters – especially cherry-pie-loving FBI Agent Dale Cooper (Kyle MacLachlan), Laura's vampy schoolmate Audrey (Sherilyn Fenn) and the infamous 'log lady' – soon become cult favourites, along with the quotable dialogue ('Diane, I'm holding in my hand a box of chocolate bunnies') and general weirdness that suffused each episode. For fans, who killed Laura Palmer was as important as 'Who shot JR?', and even when the question was answered Lynch managed to keep viewers hooked to see what other oddness would befall Cooper and Sheriff Truman (Michael Ontkean).

This box set, containing the pilot and the first seven episodes, features fascinating interviews with many of the cast and crew.

Easter Egg

Mini-Interviews

There are seven eggs (one for each episode, not including the pilot) on this disc which can be found in the following way:

Choose an episode and press ENTER.

In the episode's Main Menu, select 'Episode Features' and press ENTER.

Press the UP arrow on your remote to reveal a fire symbol in the top left-hand corner.

Press ENTER to see the following unguarded video moments with the crew:

Episode 1 – Dwayne Dunham (director/editor)

Episode 2 – Frank Byers (cinematographer)

Episode 3 – Tina Rathborne (director)

Episode 4 – Robert Engels (writer/producer)

Episode 5 – Lesli Linka Glatter (director)

Episode 6 – Caleb Deschanel (director)

Episode 7 – Harley Peyton (writer/producer)

★ ★ ★

Vanilla Sky

Based on the Spanish film *Abre los Ojos* (*Open Your Eyes*), *Vanilla Sky* is a muddled mess, but a stylish and interesting one.

The story revolves around Tom Cruise, as David, a rich, suave Manhattanite who is disfigured in a car accident, his ex-girlfriend (Cameron Diaz) and his new love (Penelope Cruz), and features director Cameron Crowe's ruminations on the meaning of life, dreams, nightmares, reality, perception and death.

While the film doesn't work on all levels – there's no chemistry between Cruise and Cruz, yet she is playing the object of his deepest obsession – we do at least get some impressive set-pieces, including an early scene in which Cruise stands utterly alone in the usually teeming Times Square (director Cameron Crowe filmed the scene in the early morning and was allowed to close down the square for shooting). There are also some great performances from the supporting cast, including Diaz, Jason Lee (as David's best friend) and Kurt Russell.

Overall, it's a bizarre, cold tale of redemption and love that never quite comes to life but still manages to hold the attention to the end credits.

Easter Egg

Gag Reel
Select 'Special Features' from the Main Menu and press ENTER.

Select 'Photo Galleries' and press ENTER.

Highlight 'Special Features' at the top of the page and press the RIGHT arrow on your remote to highlight the mask on the page.

Press ENTER for a fun five-minute collection of out-takes – you'll even get to see Tom Cruise dancing.

★ ★ ★ ★

Vertigo (Collector's Edition)

Criticised when it was first released in 1958 for its quirky plotting, this disturbing, surreal film is now rightly regarded as one of Alfred Hitchcock's masterpieces.

James Stewart is Scottie, a former cop now working as a private eye, who quit the force when his fear of heights prevented him from saving a fellow officer. Hired by Gavin Elster (Tom Elmore) to follow his blonde wife Madeleine (Kim Novak), Scottie is drawn to the unusual woman to the point of obsession, until she plummets to her death from a bell-tower. He then descends into mania when he meets a brunette doppelgänger of Madeleine named Judy (also played by Novak). With the help of new clothes and a bottle of hair dye, Scottie proceeds to transform Madeleine into a new version of Judy.

An exploration of guilt, manipulation and obsessive love, *Vertigo* is bleak but compelling, featuring two (or should that be three?) mesmerising central performances from Stewart and Novak.

Easter Egg

Alternative Ending

Select 'Bonus Materials' from the Main Menu and press ENTER.

Select 'Obsessed with Vertigo' and press ENTER.

Select 'Chapter List' and press ENTER.

Continue to the fourth page and select 'Chapter 14: Hitchcock's Foreign Censorship Ending'.

Press ENTER to access an alternative ending for the foreign release of the film. (This is the only way to access the clip.)

★ ★ ★

The Who And Special Guests Live at the Albert Hall (2 Discs)

They may have had a farewell tour in 1982, but The Who keep on going, as is evident here with their performance at London's Albert Hall in 2000 – a charity concert featuring celebrity guests such as violinist Nigel Kennedy, Oasis's Noel Gallagher, Bryan Adams, Paul Weller, Pearl Jam's Eddie Vedder and the Stereophonics' lead vocalist Kelly Jones.

Many Who classics are included in this documentary of that night, including 'The Kids Are Alright', 'Pinball Wizard', 'Who Are You', 'You Better You Bet' and, of course, 'My Generation'. Rock on …

Easter Egg

Who Fans

On Disc 1, highlight 'Program Start' and then press the RIGHT arrow on your remote to reveal 'The Who' logo on Roger Daltry's shirt.

Press ENTER for clips of the band's fans talking about seeing them in concert in November 2000.

★ ★

The Wicker Man (2-Disc Special Edition)

A spooky British horror from 1973, this has a kitsch charm that lulls you into a false sense of security before the film reveals itself as a skin-crawlingly creepy look at paganism and religion.

Sergeant Howie (Edward Woodward), a virginal, Catholic policeman from the Scottish mainland, arrives at the remote island of Summerisle to investigate the disappearance of a child. Treated as an outsider by the residents – who are alternately friendly and mysterious – Howie's investigations lead him to Lord Summerisle (Christopher Lee) himself, and the sensuous pagan rituals that take place on his estate.

After initially having its release threatened by Rod Stewart, who reportedly attempted to buy the film's negative once he discovered his girlfriend Britt Ekland appeared naked in one scene, *The Wicker Man* has deservedly won cult status over the years, and its ending remains as shocking on the tenth viewing as it was on the first.

Easter Egg

Making The Commentary

On Disc 2's Main Menu, highlight 'Commentary On' and then press the RIGHT arrow on your remote to reveal an orange figure.

Press ENTER for a fifteen-minute clip of Christopher Lee, Robin Hardy, Edward Woodward and journalist Mark Kermode recording the audio commentary for the movie in 2001.

★ ★ ★ ★

William Shakespeare's Romeo + Juliet (Special Edition)

MTV meets Shakespeare as director Baz Luhrmann (in the second of his 'Red Curtain' trilogy – *Strictly Ballroom* being the first and *Moulin Rouge!* the third) makes the Bard both cool and sexy by relocating the 400-year-old tale of tragic young love to modern-day Miami and casting two Hot Young Things (Leonardo DiCaprio and Claire Danes) as the doomed lovers. Here Verona Beach – populated by skinheads, drag queens and cool dudes – takes the place of Verona, Italy; duelling swords are replaced with guns; Juliet's nurse (the wonderful Miriam Margolyes) is now Hispanic; and sex, drugs and rock 'n' roll are everywhere.

Everything is fast, flashy, slick and backed by a thumping soundtrack (Garbage, Butthole Surfers, Radiohead) as Romeo and Juliet's romance unfolds against a backdrop of neon-lit churches, explosive gunfights and a wonderful costume-party set-piece. Happily, Luhrmann has retained most of the text while giving it sparkling new life, and his innovative direction is well served by the two beautiful, talented leads and a handsome supporting cast, which includes the powerful John Leguizamo as Tybalt, Harold Perrineau as Mercutio, and Paul Sorvino and Brian Dennehy as the heads of the Capulet and Montague dynasties. It's Shakespeare as you have never seen it before, dude.

The DVD features interviews, commentaries (by Baz Luhrmann, production designer Catherine Martin, screenwriter

Craig Pearce and director of photography Don McAlpine), plus music clips from the soundtrack.

Easter Egg

Hidden Menu And Credits

On the Main Menu, highlight 'Play' and then press the UP arrow on your remote.

This will highlight the heart at the top of the stage. Press ENTER.

This takes you to a hidden credits list and a 'Director's Gallery'. (On some versions of the DVD, this menu is also accessible via the 'Special Features' menu.)

Highlight 'Director's Gallery' and press ENTER.

There are six options to choose from:

Impact – A brief look at Luhrmann's interpretation of a classic text, and what the media thought of it.

★ ★ ★

Why Shakespeare? – Two years after its release, Luhrmann talks about why he made the movie.

★ ★ ★

Pitching Shakespeare – A very funny speech from Baz in which he explains how he pitched the movie to a Hollywood executive, this also includes clips from a video workshop he did with Leonardo DiCaprio prior to shooting.

★ ★ ★ ★

The Gas Station – The staging and shooting of the scene.

★ ★ ★ ★

The Pool Scene – The staging and shooting of the scene.

★ ★ ★ ★

Tybalt's Execution – The staging and shooting of the scene, including the car stunts.

★ ★ ★ ★

X-Men

Comic-book adaptations became cool in the new millennium with this $75-million movie directed by Bryan Singer (who'd previously made the brilliant *The Usual Suspects*).

Wolverine (Hugh Jackman), Storm (Halle Berry), Professor X (Patrick Stewart), Cyclops (James Marsden) and Dr Jean Grey (Famke Janssen) are just some of the mutants with special talents who may soon be persecuted by Senator Kelly (Bruce Davison), who believes they should all be registered rather than allowed to live incognito in society. This doesn't go down too well with Magneto (Ian McKellen), who becomes so peeved that he decides to take over the world.

The plot's a bit thin, but the effects– from Wolverine's sword-like claws that painfully emerge through his skin to Storm's impressive tricks with the climate – more than make up for it. It could be argued that McKellen, Stewart and some of the supporting cast are underused, but Jackman, who's clearly having a ball, gets a meaty role as Wolverine, while Anna Paquin provides the film's heart as the girl whose touch can put any unfortunate human in a coma.

The DVD includes deleted scenes, trailers, Hugh Jackman's screen test and featurettes.

Easter Eggs

1) *Marvel* Cameo

Select 'Special Features' from the Main Menu and press ENTER.

Select 'Theatrical Trailers and TV Spots' and press ENTER.

Highlight 'Theatrical Trailer A' and press the LEFT arrow on your remote to highlight the knight chess piece.

Press ENTER for a quick clip in which another *Marvel* comic hero sneaks into the movie.

★ ★ ★ ★

2) Character Sketches

Select 'Special Features' from the Main Menu and press ENTER.

Select 'Art Gallery' and press ENTER.

Highlight 'Main Menu' at the bottom of the page and then press the UP arrow on your remote to highlight Wolverine's dog-tags.

Press ENTER for a series of early character drawings.

★ ★ ★

Zoolander

Comic actor Ben Stiller co-wrote and directed this dumb-but-fun tale of Derek Zoolander (Stiller), the world's most dim-witted fashion model. After winning Male Model of the Year three years in a row, Zoolander is shocked when he is beaten by hot newcomer Hansel (Owen Wilson), so he prepares a comeback modelling for eccentric designer Mugatu (Will Ferrell), unaware that he is actually being brainwashed to assassinate the Prime Minister of Malaysia at a fashion event.

A deliriously daft parody of the fashion world (which takes itself far too seriously), *Zoolander* works best when Stiller is sharing scenes with his real-life father, Jerry (who plays Zoolander's agent), or digs are being made at male models, such as Zoolander describing his trademark look (which he dubs 'blue steel') or challenging Hansel to a 'walk off' in which the pair do battle by strutting their stuff down the catwalk.

The DVD includes out-takes, deleted scenes and commentary from Stiller with co-writers Drake Sather and John Hamburg.

Easter Egg

The Walk Off

Select 'Special Features' from the Main Menu and press ENTER.

On the Special Features menu select 'More' and press ENTER.

Highlight 'Photo Galleries' and press the RIGHT arrow on your remote to highlight the rotating 'M' on the screen.

Press ENTER to see Ben Stiller and Owen Wilson practising their dance moves for the 'walk off' scene in the movie. Almost as funny as the scene itself.

★ ★ ★ ★

SPOILSPORTS!

Region 1 Only DVDs

In the main reviews, I have already mentioned that Region 2 DVDs of *The Lord of the Rings: The Fellowship of the Ring* and *The Two Towers* do not contain great MTV spoofs that are on the Region 1 versions. Here are a few more eggs that you can get only on Region 1 versions of the following movies. (In the case of *The Producers*, the DVD isn't available in the UK at all!)

Boogie Nights (2-Disc New Line Platinum Series Edition)

Paul Thomas Anderson's affectionate look at porn in the 1970s – and fictional X-rated star Dirk Diggler (Mark Wahlberg) in particular – includes the following Easter egg.

Easter Egg

X-Rated Footage

On Disc 1, select 'Setup' from the Main Menu and press ENTER.

Select 'Color Bars' and press ENTER.

A test card will appear onscreen but after twenty seconds you will be treated to footage of Dirk's legendary diggler.

Dogma (2-Disc Special Edition)

Alan Rickman is an angel, Alanis Morrisette is God and Ben Affleck and Matt Damon are two renegade angels gone bad in this bonkers comic adventure from Kevin Smith, featuring his regular creations Jay (Jason Mewes) and Silent Bob (Smith himself).

Easter Eggs

1) Hidden Messages

On Disc 1, highlight 'Play Movie' on the Main Menu and then press the LEFT arrow on your remote to reveal 'Don't Play Movie'.

Press ENTER and you will get one of five messages.

2) How Jay Thinks Kevin Directs

On Disc 1, select 'Scene Selections' from the Main Menu and press ENTER.

Select 'More' and press ENTER. Continue to do this until you get to the final page of scenes.

Press '3' three times on your remote to see 'How Jay Thinks Kevin Directs', re-enacted by Jay and Silent Bob dolls.

★ ★ ★ ★

3) How Kevin Directs

On Disc 2, select 'Deleted Scenes' and press ENTER.

Select 'More' and press ENTER. Continue to do this until you get to the final page of deleted scenes.

Press '2' and then '4' to see how Kevin directs Jay, featuring Kevin Smith and Jason Mewes re-enacting their relationship on-set with dolls.

★ ★ ★ ★

Fight Club (2-Disc Special Edition)

A cinematic assault on the senses from *Se7en* director David Fincher that stars Ed Norton, Brad Pitt and Helena Bonham Carter. One assumes the reason this egg wasn't featured on the British version is because the items mentioned were only available for sale in the USA. Shame.

Easter Egg

Fight Club For Sale

On Disc 2, select 'Advertising' from the Main Menu and press ENTER.

Highlight 'Promotional Gallery' and then press the DOWN arrow on your remote to reveal a smiley face.

Press ENTER for a gallery of promotional items used for the movie.

★ ★ ★

Jay And Silent Bob Strike Back (2-Disc Dimension Collector's Edition)

The fifth film from New Jersey director Kevin Smith to feature the characters Jay (Jason Mewes) and Silent Bob (Smith), following on from *Clerks*, *Chasing Amy*, *Mallrats* and *Dogma*.

Easter Eggs

1) Jason's Balls

On Disc 2, select 'More' from the Main Menu and press ENTER to go to the second page of Special Features.

Select 'Cast and Crew Filmographies' and press ENTER.

Select 'Jason Mewes as Jay' and press ENTER.

Highlight 'Filmographies' and then press the UP arrow on your remote.

This reveals the word 'Balls'.

Press ENTER for an X-rated out-take of Mewes.

★ ★ ★

2) James L. Venable

On Disc 2, select 'More' from the Main Menu and press ENTER to go to the second page of Special Features.

Select 'Cast and Crew Filmographies' and press ENTER.

Select 'More' and press ENTER to go to the second page of filmographies.

Select 'James L Venable' and press ENTER.

Press '19' on your remote to highlight James's birthdate, and press ENTER to see a clip of the young James as a budding composer.

The Producers (Special Edition)

One of the funniest movies ever made, written and directed by Mel Brooks and featuring the comic talents of Gene Wilder and Zero Mostel as the two 'producers' trying to come up with a flop on Broadway.

Easter Eggs

1) Soundbites

Insert the 'Movie' side of the disc.

On the Main Menu, highlight 'Play Movie' and then press the LEFT arrow on your remote.

This highlights the '18' on the ticket.

Press ENTER for some soundbites from dubbing sessions for the movie.

If you then highlight '1968', '$8.50', '9', 'C' and '17' on the ticket, you will be treated to more soundbites.

★ ★ ★

2) Dancing

Highlight 'Play Movie' on the Main Menu as above.

Press the UP arrow on your remote to highlight 'Springtime for Hitler'.

Press ENTER to see animation of Lee Meredith's infamous dance as secretary Ulla from the movie.

★ ★ ★

The Sixth Sense (Collector's Edition)

Bruce Willis is the psychiatrist trying to help little Haley Joel Osment in this superbly atmospheric, spooky movie from director M. Night Shyamalan.

Easter Egg

M. Night Shyamalan's Debut

Select 'Bonus Material' from the Main Menu and press ENTER.

Select 'More' and press ENTER to go to the second page of Bonus Material.

Highlight 'Filmmaker and Cast Bios' and then press the DOWN arrow on your remote to highlight the box.

Press ENTER to see director M. Night Shyamalan introduce a clip from his first horror movie, made when he was eleven.

★ ★ ★ ★

The Usual Suspects (Special Edition)

Bryan Singer's superb whodunnit from 1995, featuring Gabriel Byrne, Benicio Del Toro, Stephen Baldwin, Kevin Pollak and Kevin Spacey as the five criminals rounded up by cop Dave Kujan (Chazz Palminteri) in his hunt for master criminal Keyser Soze.

Easter Egg

Hidden Menu

Insert the 'Special Features' side of the disc.

On the Main Menu, highlight 'Featurettes' and then press the UP arrow on your remote to highlight 'The Usual Suspects' logo.

Press ENTER and you will be taken to a screen featuring various items.

Highlight 'Quartet' and press ENTER, 'Guatemala' and ENTER, the photo of the woman and ENTER, the coffee mug and ENTER to get a secret menu.

This menu features revealing out-takes from the cast interviews, and an interview with composer and editor John Ottman.

Index

Compiled by INDEXING
SPECIALISTS (UK) LIMITED,
202 Church Road, Hove,
East Sussex BN3 2DJ.
Tel: 01273 738299